# INVESTING AND MONEY SKILLS FOR TEENAGERS

MASTER YOUR INDEPENDENCE, BUDGET
SUCCESSFULLY, AND GROW WEALTHY WITH
EASY INVESTING, REAL ESTATE STRATEGIES,
AND DOMINATE DEBT!

## CHAD K. SMITH, MBA

# TABLE OF CONTENTS

# INTRODUCTION

You have taken bold steps on a journey that many adults only dream of starting at your age. With your savings, a budget drafted, a basic understanding of your taxes, a retirement plan in place, and your first investments, you now stand at an exciting crossroads, poised to dive deeper into financial mastery. Get ready for an exhilarating quest where every choice propels you closer to conquering the art of your financial success!

In today's digital age, the internet is full of questionable financial guidance, leading many teenagers through misinformation and bewildering choices. Our education system's widespread lack of financial literacy leaves too many young people uncertain about their economic futures, vulnerable to peer influence, and prone to hasty financial decisions.

By choosing to embark on this financial journey with us, you've taken a significant step toward shaping your unique financial path. Whether your goal is to break free from the paycheck-to-paycheck cycle, set ambitious millionaire targets, achieve true financial freedom, or learn how to make your money work smarter for you,

you've made a wise and empowering choice. This book will be your trusted companion, guiding you through the intricate world of personal finance. It will help you uncover shortcuts for creating adequate budgets, learn sensible investment strategies, and gather tips for building wealth that genuinely works. As you immerse yourself in these pages, you'll deepen your financial knowledge, gaining the confidence to navigate your future with pride and discipline.

Why begin investing young? The magic of compound interest and time leverage are your secret weapons in achieving financial success. Starting in your teens opens doors to opportunities many overlook. This book simplifies the investing process, confronting common fears and dispelling myths, arming you with the insight to make savvy decisions fearlessly.

"Investing and Money Skills for Teenagers" is not just a book; it's a comprehensive guide designed to equip you with advanced financial strategies and knowledge. It goes beyond basic concepts, aiming to help you achieve financial independence. The book starts by exploring the intricacies of behavioral finance, focusing on the crucial role emotions play in investing and offering strategies for emotional discipline. It underscores the importance of cultivating a growth mindset and being mindful of peer influence in financial decisions. The chapter also introduces tools for mindful investing, ensuring that young investors like you are well-prepared to navigate your financial journeys with confidence and resilience.

As you progress through the book, you'll delve into the ever-evolving world of digital currencies and blockchain technology, gaining insights into cryptocurrency investments' high risks and potential rewards. The book continues to guide you through the complexities of global markets, sustainable investing, real estate, and diversification. It also incorporates interactive elements, such as quizzes and activities, designed to engage you actively in practical learning experiences. With chapters dedicated to advanced topics like startup investments and debt management, "Investing and Money Skills for Teenagers" provides a robust foundation for you to build and grow your wealth, equipping you with the skills necessary to navigate the dynamic world of finance.

Gear up to delve into fundamental principles, practical tips, and sophisticated concepts crafted just for the teenage investor. We'll cover everything from stock market basics to the essentials of cryptocurrency, all while keeping it engaging and relatable. Before this book, the path to financial literacy seemed filled with obstacles. Now, these challenges are simply steps on your journey to triumph.

Let this introduction be your invitation to begin an incredible investing adventure. Approach it with curiosity, a zest for learning, and the thrill of unlocking financial freedom. By the end of this journey, you'll understand the basics of investing and be prepared to stride confidently into the broader world of economic growth, no matter your starting point. This isn't just a book; it's your entry into a future where financial success is not merely a dream but an achievable reality. Welcome to the adventure of a lifetime. Let's turn the page and start this fantastic journey.

# CHAPTER 1

# FINANCIAL INDEPENDENCE QUEST:

## BEYOND THE BASICS

At the edge of a vast and unexplored financial jungle stands the aspiring investor - a teenager with eyes full of dreams and a heart brimming with ambition, the driving force behind their journey. This jungle, dense with opportunities and pitfalls, promises untold riches for those who can navigate its complexities. The key to unlocking this treasure lies not in a physical map but within one's psyche. The realm of behavioral finance offers a lantern in the dark, illuminating the path toward mastering the psychology of money management.

## 1.1 Introduction to Behavioral Finance

Behavioral finance is a fascinating branch of economics that challenges the conventional idea that people always make rational decisions to maximize their financial gain. Instead, it suggests that biases and psychological factors can lead to irrational financial behavior, such as overspending on credit cards or panic selling during market downturns. This means that our economic decisions are not always based on rationality but can be influenced by emotions and cognitive errors.

One of the most essential concepts in behavioral finance is loss aversion. This idea suggests that people are more likely to feel the pain of losing money more acutely than the pleasure of gaining it. During stock market downturns, many investors panic and sell their stocks, often at a loss, driven by fear of further financial loss. This behavior is driven by the need to avoid the pain of losing money rather than a rational analysis of the market. However, this can exacerbate the market downturn, leading to more selling and a further drop in stock prices.

Another key concept in behavioral finance is the herd mentality. This refers to people's tendency to follow a more extensive group's actions, even if it goes against their own rational analysis. During market bubbles, for example, investors may buy stocks simply because others are buying them, leading to an inflated market value not based on the company's underlying value. Similarly, during market downturns, investors may panic and sell their stocks simply because others are doing the same, leading to a self-perpetuating cycle of selling that can be difficult to break.

To sum up, behavioral finance provides insights into how our emotions can affect our financial decisions. By understanding the biases and psychological factors that lead to irrational economic behavior, we can make better decisions and avoid the pitfalls of following the crowd or being too afraid to take risks.

On the flip side, during a bull market, people can get greedy and invest a lot of money in stocks rapidly rising in value, hoping to make a quick profit. This can cause asset bubbles, where stock prices become unreasonably high compared to their actual worth. The dot-com bubble of the late 1990s and the cryptocurrency craze of recent years are examples of this phenomenon. But eventually, these bubbles burst, causing a market crash.

Behavioral finance identifies several biases that affect our financial decision-making. These include:

- Loss Aversion: People prefer to avoid losses rather than acquire gains, which can lead to selling stocks during a downturn.
- Representative Bias: Making decisions based on stereotypes or past experiences rather than the current situation.
- Overconfidence and Illusion of Control: People believe they can predict investment outcomes, leading to excessive risk-taking.
- Confirmation Bias: Seeking information confirming pre-existing beliefs leads to biased decision-making.
- Anchoring Bias: Relying too heavily on the first piece of information encountered when making decisions.
- Herding Mentality: Following the crowd when making investment decisions can lead to asset bubbles.
- Framing: Being influenced by how information is presented rather than the information itself.
- Hindsight Bias: Believing after the fact that an event was predictable and obvious.
- Narrative Fallacy: Creating a story to fit events rather than basing decisions on data.
- Self Attribution Bias: Attributing success to one's actions while blaming failure on external factors.

Understanding these biases and recognizing them in our behavior is the first step toward developing a disciplined approach to investing. Doing so allows us to make decisions based on informed strategies rather than being swayed by our emotions.

**Interactive Element: Reflective Journal Prompt**

To apply behavioral finance principles to your own life, take some time to reflect on your past financial decisions. Have you ever sold a stock in a panic during a market downturn driven by loss aversion? Or have you held onto an investment longer than you should have, convinced of its potential despite evidence to the contrary, a victim of confirmation bias?

In a journal, note these instances and the emotions that drove those decisions. Reflect on how awareness of these biases might have influenced your actions and how you can apply this understanding to future financial decisions. This exercise is not meant to judge your past actions but to develop a more critical mindset that questions instinctual reactions and seeks a deeper understanding of your financial behaviors.

This chapter aims to help you understand the psychological factors influencing financial decisions. By mastering behavioral finance, you can develop a growth-oriented financial mindset that will guide you through the complexities of the financial world and help you achieve greater prosperity.

## 1.2 The Role of Emotions in Investing

The influence of an investor's emotions on their financial decisions is a powerful force, but it also presents a significant opportunity for growth. Fear and greed, in particular, can shape market movements, but with the right strategies, investors can learn to navigate these emotions. They can learn to resist the urge to hastily offload their assets when fear takes hold, and to avoid rushing into investments for higher returns when greed prevails.

Investors' overconfidence often leads them to overvalue their knowledge and trade excessively. This behavior frequently results in impulsive decisions that can substantially damage their portfolios.

Regret is an emotion that can immobilize investors and prevent them from making necessary decisions. The fear of admitting mistakes can lead to a reluctance to sell losing positions, and the anticipation of regret can prevent them from taking necessary risks.

Investors have a limited attention span, and abundant information is available, making it difficult to focus on relevant data and make informed investment decisions. This often leads to a reliance on heuristics and superficial assessments, resulting in a portfolio that needs more solid foundations.

Chasing trends is an example of the herd mentality that can grip investors. The misconception that past performance indicates future results perpetuates this cycle of euphoria and despair.

Emotional discipline is a cornerstone of successful investing. Maintaining composure in market volatility and approaching investing with a measured analytical mindset are essential. This discipline sets successful investors apart from those who are controlled by their emotions.

Investors can fortify their defenses against the psychological pitfalls that can hinder financial success. Through introspection, education, and the cultivation of emotional resilience, investors can take control of their investment decisions. This resilience is a powerful tool, enabling investors to bounce back from losses and setbacks, and to make decisions based on reason rather than emotion. In this endeavor, the investor is both the sculptor and the marble, shaped by market forces but capable of transcending them through determination and self-mastery.

## 1.3 Strategies for Emotional Discipline

Keeping your emotions in check is essential for making smart money moves in the world of investing. This chapter will equip you with the tools to stay calm and focused, even when the market seems like a wild ride. Think of it like steering a ship through rough waters—you need a steady hand, a clear plan, and the ability to stick to your course no matter what.

### Setting Long-Term Goals

The foundation of emotional discipline lies in setting long-term objectives. These goals act as your anchor during market ups and downs, helping you focus on building wealth steadily over time instead of getting caught up in short-term wins or losses. Every investment you make should be a building block in your financial future, creating a solid foundation that can weather any storm.

### Limiting Market Monitoring

One of the biggest emotional traps in investing is the urge to check the market constantly. Obsessively watching your portfolio can lead to stress and impulsive decisions driven by excitement or fear. By setting a regular schedule for portfolio reviews, you give your investments the space they need to grow, allowing you to maintain a calm and balanced approach.

## Crafting a Financial Plan

Having a solid financial plan is like having a blueprint for success. It helps you navigate the complex world of investing with confidence, turning what might seem like risky bets into calculated decisions. A well-thought-out plan also enables you to identify which opportunities are worth pursuing and which are too dangerous, protecting you from the lure of high-stakes gambles.

## Leveraging Automation

Incorporating automation into your investment strategy can be a game-changer for maintaining emotional discipline. Tools like automatic contributions to your investment accounts or robo-advisors for portfolio management remove emotion from decision-making. By following predefined criteria, these tools help ensure that your investments are based on logic and long-term goals, not fleeting emotions.

## Thinking Ahead

Emotional discipline also means looking to the future and considering the possible outcomes of each investment decision. By studying historical trends and imagining different future scenarios, you can better prepare yourself for whatever the market throws. This forward-thinking approach helps you navigate uncertainty with confidence.

## Managing Regret

Fear of regret can be a powerful force in decision-making. By acknowledging this emotion and carefully weighing the potential for regret against the benefits of an investment, you can make more balanced choices. This strategy helps you avoid being swayed by the fear of what might go wrong, allowing you to focus on what's most likely to go right.

### Seeking Diverse Perspectives

No one has all the answers, so seeking advice from trusted experts with different experiences and viewpoints is essential. Engaging with diverse perspectives helps you see potential blind spots and challenges your assumptions, leading to better, more informed decisions.

### Embracing Automation

Investing can be an emotional rollercoaster, but there's a way to add more discipline to your process—automation. By automating your financial choices, you protect your strategies from impulsive decisions and ensure your investment activities align with your long-term goals. Whether setting up automatic contributions or using robo-advisors for portfolio rebalancing, automation provides a steadying influence that reduces the risk of making hasty, regrettable decisions.

### The Challenge of Emotional Discipline

Achieving emotional discipline in investing is challenging. It requires a deep understanding of the relationship between psychology and finance and a commitment to self-awareness. It would help if you were willing to confront your biases and develop a mindset prioritizing rationality and long-term thinking over short-term temptations.

In this journey, you are both the navigator and the vessel, charting a course through the turbulent market waters with a compass set to the true north of disciplined decision-making. So, don't let your emotions steer you off course. Embrace automation, stay focused on your goals, and take control of your investment journey.

## 1.4 Developing a Growth Mindset

When it comes to money, having a growth mindset is essential for achieving long-term success. It's all about believing you can develop your abilities and intelligence with hard work and dedication. This mindset allows you to deal with financial challenges and helps you see that financial skills can be learned over time. Instead of focusing on your limitations, a growth mindset encourages you to keep improving.

To understand how a growth mindset can help you with your finances, you must challenge your preconceptions about money. Ask yourself: "What is money to me?" Your answer will reflect your beliefs about wealth, often influenced by your family and society. Your beliefs about money can either help you grow financially or hold you back in a cycle of scarcity.

To develop a growth mindset regarding finances, you must be resilient and adaptable. This means seeing challenges as opportunities to learn, not as roadblocks. A growth mindset helps you learn from mistakes, like losing money on an investment or needing help with a budget. Instead of feeling like a failure, you see these setbacks as valuable lessons to help you improve next time.

Feedback is important for developing a growth mindset, even if it seems like criticism. Being open to constructive criticism from others or reflecting on your own progress can help you grow. Feedback can help you refine your strategies and broaden your perspective. Being willing to listen to feedback shows you're more interested in increasing than protecting your ego.

A growth mindset helps you overcome the fear of failure, which can hold you back from taking risks or trying new things with your money. Instead of seeing failure as a reason to give up, a growth mindset helps you see failure as a natural part of the learning process. This encourages you to explore different investment strategies, try new ways of budgeting, and seek out financial education, knowing that every mistake is a step toward success.

Cultivating a growth mindset takes perseverance, especially when it comes to finances. You must be willing to keep trying, even when things get tough. Every effort, decision, and setback is a step towards greater financial wisdom, and it's essential to remember that. Success isn't just for the lucky few—it can be achieved through hard work and dedication.

Finally, having an open mind is essential when it comes to developing a growth mindset. You must be willing to step outside your comfort zone, consider new investment ideas, and adapt your strategies as the financial landscape changes. Being open to new possibilities allows for innovation and helps you discover unique ways to grow wealth.

In short, having a growth mindset regarding your finances means believing in yourself, being open to feedback, learning from your mistakes, and being willing to keep trying, even when things get tough. It's all about seeing the potential for growth and success rather than focusing on your limitations and fears.

Embracing a growth mindset in personal finance and investing does not negate the reality of financial risk or the complexity of market forces. Instead, it equips individuals with the psychological tools to engage with these challenges constructively. It encourages a proactive stance towards learning, an openness to feedback, and a resilience that transforms setbacks into springboards for growth. This mindset does not promise a path devoid of obstacles. Still, it offers the assurance that each obstacle encountered is an opportunity to advance further on the journey to financial mastery.

In this light, developing a growth mindset is not merely a psychological exercise but a practical strategy for financial empowerment. It acknowledges that the most potent asset in one's financial portfolio is not a particular stock or investment but the mindset one approaches the financial world.

## 1.5 The Impact of Peer Influence

Social media and peer groups significantly influence investment decisions in today's financial landscape. People often feel pressured to conform to their friends' financial habits, choices, and social media connections. Social media platforms are particularly influential in this regard, as individuals try to curate their online image and win the approval of their audience. People often feel envious and discontented with their own lives after seeing the curated lifestyles of others online. This can lead to a desire to elevate one's lifestyle at the expense of financial prudence.

Conversations with peers can also skew perceptions of investing. People may hear about leveraged investments in volatile markets or the latest speculative asset and think of them as high-stakes gambles for immediate gratification rather than a disciplined march toward long-term financial security. The allure of joining the ranks of those who seemingly struck gold overnight can be tempting. Still, it often leads to economic instability in the long run.

The most significant danger of being influenced by others in financial matters is not the immediate monetary loss but the gradual erosion of independent thinking. Constant exposure to the economic successes of others and the materialistic world can cloud judgment and lead to a herd mentality. This results in decisions not based on thorough research or personal financial planning but on a fear of missing out on the next big thing. This shift from autonomy to reacting to societal trends and peer actions is a dangerous pivot that can compromise one's financial security.

The solution to this pervasive influence is not to disconnect from the digital world or cut ties with one's social circle but to cultivate a mindset of skepticism and self-reliance. This involves critically evaluating the sources of financial advice and being committed to personal financial goals. It starts with recognizing the influence of peers and social media and filtering their inputs through rational thought.

To do this effectively, one must clearly understand their financial situation and objectives. They must set measurable goals and develop a roadmap to achieve them, independent of external approval and societal benchmarks of success. This clarity serves as a shield against envy and impulsive financial decisions.

Additionally, it's helpful to surround oneself with people with diverse experiences and thoughts. This helps to challenge consensus and enrich one's perspective. This creates an environment where economic decisions are discussed and analyzed rather than blindly followed. Through respectful discussions and a shared pursuit of financial wisdom, individuals can gain the insights necessary to navigate the complexities of investing.

In today's world, social media significantly impacts our financial decisions. However, we can reduce this influence by deliberately curating our digital environment. This involves consciously selecting online communities focusing on financial education and investing, where substance is more important than spectacle. Such forums provide a space for learning and growth, where investors can find a bulwark against the tide of sensationalism. Here, discussions are anchored in data and analysis, which helps investors acquire knowledge and improve their investment acumen.

The path to financial independence is not about isolation but selective engagement. Investors should evaluate the voices of peers and social media with a critical eye rather than blindly following them. By doing so, they can emerge not as a leaf tossed by the winds of influence but as a navigator, charting a course based on personal convictions and informed choices. The challenge lies in maintaining this course, steadfast in the face of the siren songs of conformity and immediate gratification. It requires resilience, a commitment to self-education, and the courage to stand apart when prudence dictates. Investors who successfully navigate these waters can craft a portfolio and a legacy of financial autonomy and wisdom.

## 1.6 Tools for Mindful Investing

In the digital age, the investor's arsenal brims with tools and platforms designed to illuminate the path of financial growth, offering clarity in a complex realm. The prudent selection and utilization of these digital companions can transform investing from a source of undue stress to a disciplined pursuit of prosperity. Yet, the key lies not in the abundance of these tools but in their judicious application, ensuring they serve as instruments of enlightenment rather than conduits of anxiety.

Among the plethora of available applications, YNAB (You Need A Budget) emerges as a beacon for those seeking mastery over their finances through zero-based budgeting principles. This approach, meticulous in its demand that every dollar be assigned a purpose, fosters a thorough awareness of one's financial flow. YNAB's intuitive yet comprehensive interface encourages hands-on engagement with one's budget, transforming abstract financial goals into tangible, actionable plans.

Parallel to the granular control offered by YNAB, Goodbudget presents a digital incarnation of the envelope budgeting system. This time-honored strategy allocates funds to categorized envelopes each month. This method, grounded in the physical separation of resources to curb overspending, finds new life in Goodbudget's platform. Here, the virtual envelopes provide a visual snapshot of financial health, allowing users to navigate their spending habits with precision and foresight.

For those seeking simplicity in their budgeting endeavors, Every-Dollar offers a streamlined approach. This platform, founded on the principles of Dave Ramsey's financial philosophy, emphasizes the power of planning in achieving financial freedom. Its interface, devoid of unnecessary complexity, allows users to create a budget in mere minutes, underscoring the accessibility of economic management to all, regardless of their prior experience or expertise.

Beyond budgeting, Empower Personal Wealth emerges as a comprehensive tool for tracking spending and the entire financial landscape. Empower consolidates financial data from investments to savings into a unified dashboard, offering insights that span the breadth of one's financial journey. This holistic view, enriched with analytics and personalized recommendations, guides users toward informed decisions and strategic adjustments.

In investment tracking, the landscape is equally rich with platforms designed to demystify market movements and portfolio performance. SigFig Wealth Management, for instance, offers an elegant solution for monitoring investments, providing users with a detailed analysis of their portfolio's composition, performance, and fees. This transparency, paired with personalized investment advice, equips investors with the knowledge to refine their strategies in alignment with their financial goals.

Sharesight, another notable contender, specializes in tracking stocks, mutual funds, and ETFs across multiple portfolios. Its capability to capture dividends, capital gains, and losses in real-time offers a granular view of investment performance, shedding light on the nuances that shape financial outcomes. Moreover, Sharesight's tax reporting features streamline the often-dreaded tax preparation process, providing investors with a comprehensive overview of their taxable income and potential deductions.

The Yahoo! Finance App, renowned for its broad accessibility, is a gateway to real-time market data, news, and analysis. Its utility extends beyond mere observation, enabling users to confidently act on insights. The app's integration of customizable alerts ensures that investors remain abreast of significant market developments, allowing for timely adjustments to their investment strategies.

As the financial landscape evolves, so do the tools at the investor's disposal. The emergence of platforms like Honeydue, which cater to the unique financial dynamics of couples, underscores the expanding scope of digital financial tools. Honeydue facilitates shared budgeting and savings goals, fostering transparency and collaboration in financial planning. This approach, recognizing the shared nature of financial responsibilities among partners, underscores the importance of communication and joint strategizing in achieving financial harmony.

The mindful application of these tools, each carefully designed to illuminate aspects of the financial landscape, requires a discerning eye. It is not merely the adoption of technology that empowers the investor but the strategic integration of these platforms into a cohesive financial plan. This plan, informed by real-time data and analytics, becomes a living document, adaptable to the shifting sands of the market and the evolving aspirations of the investor.

In this digital era, the investor is no longer a solitary figure navigating the financial wilderness with intuition as their sole guide. Instead, they stand at the helm of a sophisticated command center equipped with tools that offer visibility and insight into the complex interplay of market forces. When wielded with intention and discernment, these platforms transform the act of investing into a disciplined pursuit of growth grounded in mindfulness and strategic planning principles.

The journey through the financial landscape, enriched with the capabilities afforded by modern technology, becomes not just a quest for wealth but a voyage of discovery. Here, amid the ebb and flow of markets and the ever-present challenge of financial decision-making, the investor finds a path to clarity. This clarity, born of data and analysis, is the foundation upon which financial dreams are built and realized.

## 1.7 Overview & Final Thoughts About this Chapter

In attaining financial wisdom, a meticulously kept journal serves not merely as a repository of actions taken but as a mirror reflecting the interplay between emotion and logic that guides these decisions. This document, a ledger of the mind's negotiations with the heart, becomes a tool for self-examination, offering insights into the undercurrents that influence your financial behaviors. The creation of such a journal, therefore, is not a task undertaken lightly but a disciplined exercise in self-awareness and growth!

To initiate this process, the investor begins by dedicating a physical or digital space explicitly reserved for this endeavor. This space, free from the clutter of daily life, becomes a sanctuary for reflection. Here, each entry starts with a description of a financial decision, whether an investment made, a budget adjusted, or a purchase contemplated. A detailed, yet succinct description sets the stage for the following deeper analysis.

Following this, the investor annotates what motivated the decision. This annotation seeks to uncover the layers beneath the surface, discerning whether the choice stemmed from a well-reasoned strategy or a fleeting emotion. Was it the thrill of potential gain that tipped the scales, or was it a carefully constructed plan aimed at long-term growth? Perhaps it was fear, a specter whispering of impending losses, that guided the hand. Or it was confidence, bolstered by research and analysis, that led the way. This introspection, though it may uncover uncomfortable truths, is invaluable. It lays bare the rational and emotional forces that shape financial paths.

Next, the outcome of the decision is recorded with unflinching honesty. Whether it chronicles success or setback, this record is not a judgment but an observation. It serves as a testament to the reality that not all well-founded decisions bear fruit, nor do all emotional impulses lead to ruin. Here, in the aftermath of action, lies the learning opportunity. The investor examines the divergence between expectation and reality, seeking lessons in the chasm between.

The final step in this reflective process is synthesizing what was learned. This synthesis, a distillation of experience into wisdom, is the most crucial element of the journal. Here, patterns emerge, revealing tendencies towards overconfidence or undue caution. Here, strategies are refined and honed by the dual forces of success and failure. And it is here that growth occurs, as the investor iterates on their approach, informed by the past but not tethered to it.

Though personal and private, this journal need not be a solitary endeavor. The investor might seek the counsel of mentors or peers, sharing insights gleaned to illuminate common pitfalls and strategies. This sharing, a confluence of diverse experiences, enriches the individual journey with collective wisdom. It transforms the journal from a mere log of transactions into a dynamic tool for communal learning and growth.

Moreover, the investor integrates this reflective practice into their financial routine, regularly revisiting the journal. This periodic review, a ritual, ensures that the lessons are preserved with time. It allows the investor to track their evolution, noting shifts in perspective and strategy as they navigate the financial landscape. Over months and years, this tracking portrays the investor's journey, marked by growth, adaptation, and wisdom.

As the entries accumulate, the journal becomes a testament to the investor's journey, a tangible record of the intersection between emotion, logic, and financial decision-making. It is a constant reminder of the financial world's complexity and the nuanced approach required to navigate it successfully. Through this document, the investor gains insight into their financial behaviors and charts a course for future growth, informed by the rich tapestry of past experiences.

In this way, the journal transcends its function as a mere tool for reflection, becoming a compass by which the investor steers their course through the tumultuous seas of the financial world. It stands as a beacon of self-awareness, guiding the investor towards a future where decisions are made not in the shadow of emotion, but in the light of informed deliberate strategy. This process, iterative and evolving, mirrors the essence of the financial journey itself —a journey marked not by the destination but by the wisdom gained along the way.

# CHAPTER 2
# THE DIGITAL CURRENCY EXPEDITION:
## DECRYPTING CRYPTOCURRENCIES

C ryptocurrencies are pioneers in a sweeping financial revolution in the ever-evolving landscape where the tangible meets the intangible. Envision a vibrant marketplace where transactions are instant, boundless, and crystal precise, yet no physical exchange occurs. Fueled by the art of cryptography, this domain has radically altered our understanding of money, challenging the very bedrock of traditional banking systems. Embark on this digital currency expedition with us as we unravel the complexities of cryptocurrencies and blockchain technology, uncovering their vast potential to redefine our financial future.

The birth of Bitcoin marks a historic milestone, igniting a new epoch of digital currency that thrives free from centralized oversight. In contrast to fiat currencies, controlled by national banks and vulnerable to inflation, cryptocurrencies present a decentralized alternative. They operate on blockchain technology, a digital ledger that meticulously records transactions across a global network of computers, ensuring unmatched security and transparency.

**Introduction to Cryptocurrencies**

Cryptocurrencies are fundamentally different from traditional money. They exist solely in digital form, secured in digital wallets, and are exchanged directly between peers, bypassing the need for intermediaries like banks. This system speeds up transactions and slashes the costs tied to international money transfers. Unlike fiat currencies, whose supply can be manipulated by governmental policies, the quantity of cryptocurrencies is fixed by intricate algorithms, creating a scarcity that can drive their value.

Globally, the acceptance of cryptocurrencies varies—some nations recognize them as valid payment methods. In contrast, others restrict or completely ban them due to concerns about security and illicit activities. The volatility of cryptocurrencies is a double-edged sword, offering the prospect of substantial returns but also entailing considerable risks for investors.

One can only explore the realm of cryptocurrencies by acknowledging Bitcoin, conceived by the mysterious Satoshi Nakamoto. Bitcoin introduced the world to decentralized currency and set the groundwork for countless other cryptocurrencies.

Other notable cryptocurrencies like Ethereum, Ripple, Solana, and Cardano have built on Bitcoin's legacy, each adding unique innovations. Ethereum, for example, transcends being just a currency by facilitating decentralized applications through smart contracts. Ripple targets the banking sector, aiming to revolutionize international transfers to be quicker and cheaper. Litecoin, often dubbed the silver to Bitcoin's gold, boasts speedier transaction times and a larger supply limit.

Those delving into cryptocurrency investments begin by choosing a credible exchange. Platforms such as Coinbase and Crypto.com are renowned for their reliability in trading digital currencies. After securing an account, investors can acquire cryptocurrencies, storing them in hardware wallets for peak security or software wallets for convenience.

Maintaining rigorous security practices is crucial in the cryptocurrency sphere. Regular backups, prudent sharing of private keys, and alertness against phishing are vital to protect your digital assets. Keeping abreast of the dynamic field of cryptocurrency security and updates is equally essential.

Thorough personal research is imperative before investing in cryptocurrency. This principle, emphasized in the crypto community, highlights the necessity of understanding a cryptocurrency's purpose, the team behind it, and its market prospects. Imagine a college student allocating a portion of their savings to cryptocurrencies. They dedicate weeks to studying various options, evaluating the market, and finally choosing a blend of established and emerging digital currencies, safeguarding their investment in a hardware wallet. Over time, they continuously monitor their portfolio using apps like Delta, adjusting their strategy based on performance and ongoing research. While platforms like Uphold, eToro, and CoinStats offer tools for monitoring investments and staying current with market trends, there are other platforms that might better suit their needs. For example, Binance and Coinbase Pro offer advanced trading features and lower fees for active traders, while Gemini provides strong security measures and a user-friendly interface. Kraken is known for its wide range of supported cryptocurrencies and robust security features. Depending on your investment goals, it might be worth exploring these options to find the platform that best aligns with your needs. However, if you are a U.S. citizen, be aware that some crypto exchanges are not fully approved by regulatory authorities, so make sure to verify their legal standing within your country before proceeding.

The journey of investing in cryptocurrency, like the college student's dedication, is a testament to the power of informed decision-making and the courage to step into new financial frontiers. Remember, every move you make is a step toward not just financial growth, but personal growth—building the discipline, knowledge, and resilience that will serve you well beyond your investments. Keep pushing forward, stay curious, and let your passion for learning guide you to success.

## Ethical and Social Implications

The ascent of cryptocurrencies also illuminates ethical and social issues. The significant energy demands of mining activities, especially for Bitcoin, prompt environmental concerns. Initiatives are in place to transition to more sustainable consensus mechanisms like proof-of-stake, which Ethereum has adopted. Furthermore, cryptocurrencies promise to enhance global financial inclusion by providing alternative banking solutions to unbanked populations worldwide.

Beyond finance, blockchain technology revolutionizes sectors like supply chain management by ensuring transparency and traceability from production to delivery. In electoral systems, blockchain presents a secure, tamper-proof method for vote recording, proclaiming a future of more transparent and fair elections! Can you imagine this future? This technology validates and authenticates each vote through a decentralized ledger, ensuring every ballot is counted and verified like never before. Instead of just getting a sticker and hoping that our vote counts, blockchain represents the integrity of our future society, guaranteeing that our voices are heard and protected. Join us as we navigate this transformative journey through the digital frontier of finance, where innovation meets trust and the future of democracy is secured through technology.

## 2.1 Interactive Element: Cryptocurrency Quiz

To test your understanding of cryptocurrencies and blockchain technology, take this quiz:

### What mechanism does Bitcoin use to secure its blockchain?

- *Bitcoin uses a consensus mechanism called Proof of Work (PoW) to secure its blockchain. This involves miners solving complex mathematical puzzles to validate and add new blocks to the blockchain.*

### Name three critical differences between cryptocurrencies and fiat currencies.

- *Decentralization vs. Centralization: Cryptocurrencies are typically decentralized and operate on a blockchain, while fiat currencies are centralized and controlled by governments or central banks.*
- *Supply Control: The supply of most cryptocurrencies is fixed or algorithmically controlled, whereas fiat currencies can be printed and regulated by central banks, leading to potential inflation.*
- *Digital vs. Physical Form: Cryptocurrencies exist solely in digital form and are transferred electronically, while fiat currencies can exist both as physical cash (coins and banknotes) and digital money in bank accounts.*

### Which cryptocurrency introduced intelligent contracts?

- *Ethereum introduced smart contracts, which are self-executing contracts with the terms of the agreement directly written into code.*

**What environmental concern is associated with cryptocurrency mining?**

- *The primary environmental concern is the high energy consumption associated with cryptocurrency mining, especially for those using Proof of Work (PoW) mechanisms like Bitcoin, which require vast amounts of computational power and electricity. This has raised concerns about the carbon footprint and sustainability of mining operations.*

Exploiting cryptocurrencies and blockchain technology reveals a frontier teeming with potential and pitfalls. As digital currencies evolve, their impact on the global financial system and society remains intensely studied and debated. With knowledge and a critical mindset, investors can navigate this digital financial landscape, poised to capitalize on its opportunities while mindful of the risks.

## 2.2 Understanding Blockchain Mechanics

In an era when digitization of everything from communication to currency has become the norm, blockchain technology emerges as the bedrock of this new digital frontier. Imagine a world where every transaction, regardless of its nature, gets chronicled not in some dusty ledger hidden away in a bank vault but on a network that is everywhere and nowhere. This is the realm of blockchain, a decentralized ledger that forgoes the need for traditional intermediaries, rewiring the very architecture of financial transactions and beyond.

At its core, blockchain technology is a distributed database. This ledger maintains an ever-expanding list of records known as blocks. Each block is connected to the preceding one through a cryptographic hash, forming an unbreakable chain. The essence of blockchain's ingenuity lies in its decentralization. Rather than residing on a single server or location, copies of the blockchain exist across a network of computers, each node holding a complete copy of the ledger. This decentralization renders the blockchain impervious to manipulation, ensuring the integrity of each recorded transaction.

The implications of such a system are profound. In a stroke, blockchain technology obliterates the need for the financial gate-keepers that have long dominated our transactions. Individuals no longer must rely on banks or other financial institutions to validate their exchanges. Instead, this responsibility is distributed across the network, with each node working together to confirm transactions through consensus mechanisms. This shift democratizes financial transactions and significantly enhances their efficiency and security.

The security afforded by blockchain technology is unparalleled. Given its decentralized nature, altering any record within the blockchain would require an impossible consensus across the entire network. Each block's cryptographic hash, a digital finger-print, further fortifies the chain. Any attempt to tamper with the data within a block would alter its hash, breaking the chain and alerting the network to the anomaly. This cryptographic chaining and the network's consensus mechanisms ensure it is virtually immutable once a transaction is recorded on the blockchain.

Transparency, another cornerstone of blockchain technology, fosters an environment of trust. While the parties' identities can be shielded, the transaction is visible to anyone within the network. This transparency ensures accountability, a particularly enticing feature for applications beyond financial transactions, such as supply chain management or voting systems.

Eliminating intermediaries through blockchain technology heralds a new era of efficiency and cost reduction. Traditional financial transactions, especially those crossing borders, can be bogged down by bureaucratic red tape and exorbitant fees. Blockchain technology, by contrast, enables swift, direct exchanges between parties, irrespective of geographical boundaries. This acceleration of transactions, devoid of intermediary fees, not only enhances accessibility but also opens the door to a global marketplace truly without borders.

A simple diagram illustrating the workings of blockchain technology might depict a series of blocks, each containing transaction data, a timestamp, and a cryptographic hash. These blocks are connected linearly, with each hash pointing to the previous block, forming a chain. This visualization conveys the essence of blockchain's security and integrity, illustrating how each block component contributes to the ledger's inviolability.

The benefits of blockchain extend well beyond its foundational role in cryptocurrencies. In business, blockchain technology promises a revolution in transparency and efficiency. Trust, often a scarce commodity in transactions, becomes inherent within a blockchain's structure. Its decentralized architecture distributes control, mitigating the risks associated with centralized data storage and management. The result is a system where security and privacy are not mutually exclusive but are instead intertwined, each transaction reinforcing the network's integrity.

Moreover, blockchain's capacity for reducing costs, both in terms of transactions and operations, is a game-changer for businesses. By automating processes traditionally requiring manual intervention and verification, blockchain technology streamlines operations, freeing resources to be allocated elsewhere. Its application in supply chain management exemplifies this, with blockchain providing real-time visibility into the journey of goods from manufacturer to consumer. This visibility enhances efficiency and builds consumer trust, a currency of immeasurable value in the digital age.

Innovation thrives on the blockchain, and its flexibility and security provide a fertile ground for developing new applications. From tokenization, which allows tangible assets to be represented digitally on the blockchain, to intelligent contracts that execute automatically upon meeting predefined conditions, blockchain technology is redefining the possible. These applications, each leveraging the blockchain's unique properties, hint at a future where digital and physical merge, reshaping industries and society in ways yet to be fully realized.

As the blockchain continues to evolve, its potential applications expand, limited only by the imagination of those who seek to harness its power. In this digital odyssey, the blockchain is the vessel and the voyage. This technology promises not just to change the way we transact but to redefine the very notion of value in the digital age.

## 2.3 High Risks & the Potential of Digital Currencies

In the dynamic weave of modern finance, cryptocurrencies blaze with electrifying potential, threading together the promise of groundbreaking innovation with the thrill of navigating uncharted risks. This exhilarating duality creates a high-stakes landscape for investors, where the pulse-pounding challenges of currencies and regulatory uncertainty match the dazzling allure of digital currencies' transformative power.

Cryptocurrencies are like digital money that can be used anywhere worldwide without relying on slow and expensive traditional banks. They make it easier and faster to buy things, send money, and invest, all while using blockchain's secure technology to keep everything safe. This technology not only makes transactions transparent but also holds the potential to change the way we handle money in the future.

Investing in cryptocurrencies is exciting because they can grow in value very quickly, offering a chance to make a lot of money. They also help protect against inflation when regular cash loses value over time. However, it's essential to understand that roughly 95% of crypto assets will not make it in the long run, meaning many could lose their value entirely. This makes it super important for everyone to do their own research before diving into them. Cryptocurrencies can be very unpredictable—their prices can go up or down suddenly, which means you could lose money as quickly as you could make it.

Another thing to remember is that governments are still figuring out the rules about cryptocurrencies. Some countries support them, while others are more cautious or ban them. This uncertainty can make investing in cryptocurrencies even riskier.

Security is another big concern. Although blockchain is designed to be secure, the digital nature of cryptocurrencies means they can be targets for hackers. There have been cases where people lost a lot of money because of cyber-attacks, so protecting your investments with solid security measures is crucial.

On the flip side, there are stories of people who have made huge profits by investing in cryptocurrencies early on. But there are also stories of people who lost everything because they invested without fully understanding the risks.

To invest wisely in cryptocurrencies, you must research and stay informed about how the market works. It's a high-risk, high-reward game; only those who are prepared and cautious will come out on top.

Interestingly, Larry Fink, the CEO of BlackRock, has spoken about how blockchain technology could eventually tokenize everything. This means that, in the future, we might see assets like real estate, stocks, and even votes being recorded and verified on the blockchain. Instead of just hoping our votes or transactions are counted, blockchain could ensure that everything is done fairly and transparently. This could be a huge step forward for truth within our societies, ensuring that what matters most is protected and trustworthy.

## 2.4 How to Get Started with Cryptocurrency Investments

In the realm of digital finance, getting started with cryptocurrency investments is like a carefully choreographed dance, involving deliberate steps to navigate the complexities of this growing field. Venturing into this space requires a willingness to take risks and a disciplined approach to protecting one's digital assets. Here, we provide a guide to help those ready to step into the world of digital currency investment.

### Step 1: Choose a Cryptocurrency Exchange

The gateway to the cryptographic realm begins with selecting a cryptocurrency exchange, a digital marketplace where currencies like Bitcoin and Ethereum are bought and sold. This crucial decision hinges on the exchange's reputation for security and customer service—key features of platforms like Coinbase and Crypto.com. These trusted exchanges have successfully navigated the challenges of cyber threats, earning the confidence of the crypto community. Their user-friendly interfaces cater to both beginners and experienced investors, making it easier to navigate the complex world of cryptocurrency trading. However, if you are a U.S. citizen, be aware that regulatory authorities do not entirely approve some crypto exchanges. It's vital to verify the legal standing of the exchange within your country before proceeding to ensure your investments are secure and compliant.

### Step 2: Set Up and Secure Your Account

Once you've chosen an exchange, the next step is to create and secure your account with the precision and care of a locksmith crafting a key. Start by creating a strong, unique password—this is your first line of defense against unauthorized access. This password, which you have full control over, is a crucial step in securing your account. But don't stop there. Activating two-factor authentication (2FA) is essential; it adds a powerful second layer of security, acting as a cryptographic shield to protect your digital assets. This simple but effective security measure is crucial in safeguarding your investments from cyber threats. Taking the time to set up 2FA is highly encouraged, as it significantly reduces the risk of your account being compromised!

### Step 3: Purchase Cryptocurrency

Now comes the exciting part—buying your first cryptocurrency! Think of this as your ticket into the future of finance. But before you dive in, there's a crucial step: verification. While a bit tedious, this process is super important because it ensures that everything is above board and compliant with the rules. Once verified, you can explore the marketplace and decide which digital currency to invest in. Whether you choose Bitcoin, Ethereum, or something new and up-and-coming, this moment marks your entry into the thrilling world of cryptocurrencies.

### Step 4: Choose a Wallet for Storage

Once you've got your crypto, the next step is keeping it safe. Just like you wouldn't carry much cash in your pocket, you shouldn't leave your digital assets on an exchange. Instead, you'll need a secure wallet to store your cryptocurrency. There are two main types of wallets: hardware and software. A hardware wallet is like a digital safe you can hold, giving you top-notch security. On the other hand, a software wallet is super convenient and easy to access online, perfect if you plan on using your crypto regularly. Choosing the right wallet is all about finding the balance between security and convenience that works for you.

### Step 5: Transfer Cryptocurrency to Your Wallet

With your wallet ready, it's time to move your cryptocurrency from the exchange to its new home. This step is crucial—think of it as transferring your treasure to a secure vault. Just ensure you get the address right, as a small mistake could send your assets entirely elsewhere! Once the transfer is complete, you've fully controlled your investment.

### Step 6: Secure Your Wallet

Now that your cryptocurrency is safely stored, it's time to lock it down. You will be given a recovery phrase for hardware wallets—a set of words that act as your master key. Write this down and keep it somewhere safe because if you lose your wallet, this phrase is your only way to get your crypto back. Use strong, unique passwords for software wallets, and consider installing antivirus software to guard against online threats.

### Step 7: Maintain Security Practices

Security doesn't stop once your wallet is set up—it's an ongoing process. Regularly back up your wallet to avoid losing assets if something goes wrong. Keep your private keys and recovery phrases hidden, and never share them with anyone. Be on the lookout for phishing scams and suspicious links, and always trust your instincts—if something feels off, it probably will be off!

### Step 8: Keep Informed and Updated

The world of cryptocurrency is constantly changing, so staying informed is essential. Keep up with the latest news, updates, and security practices to protect your investment. Make it a habit to check in with your wallet provider and stay up-to-date on any new features or security enhancements. Staying informed will help you make smart decisions and keep your assets safe.

In this journey into the world of cryptocurrencies, you're not just investing but becoming a part of the future. By following these steps, you're taking control of your financial destiny with confidence and strategy. With each move you make, you're not just diving into digital currency; you're safeguarding your future with the wisdom and foresight of a seasoned pro. Keep learning, stay vigilant, and embrace the exciting possibilities ahead!

### 2.5 Ethical and Social Implications

In today's fast-changing world of finance, where digital currencies are creating new opportunities, it's important to think about the bigger picture and the responsibilities that come with these innovations. While cryptocurrencies are shaking things up and opening doors, we need to consider some important ethical issues—like the environmental impact of the energy used in blockchain technology. It's up to us to find ways to make these processes more eco-friendly, like shifting to energy-efficient methods, so we can enjoy the benefits of these technologies without harming the planet.

As we explore this exciting world, keeping our moral compass pointed in the right direction is crucial. Investing in cryptocurrencies shouldn't just be about chasing quick profits but understanding their broader impact on society. Sure, there's a thrill in seeing your investments grow, but it's also about using this technology to make a positive difference. By staying informed and practicing moderation, we can avoid the pitfalls of speculative trading and focus on responsible, sustainable investing.

On a global scale, there's a growing need for clear rules and regulations to guide how cryptocurrencies fit into the traditional financial system. These guidelines are important not just for keeping things fair and preventing illegal activities but also for protecting investors from the market's ups and downs. As innovation continues, these regulations will help ensure that everyone can participate safely and securely.

Reducing blockchain technology's environmental impact is a powerful example of how we can balance digital innovation with caring for our planet. By moving towards energy-efficient methods, the blockchain community can significantly reduce its carbon footprint, showing that we can be tech-savvy and eco-conscious simultaneously.

But the potential of blockchain goes way beyond just digital currencies—it's set to transform industries like supply chain management, where it can bring unprecedented transparency and accountability. Imagine a world where every step of a product's journey is visible and secure, reducing the risk of counterfeit goods and ensuring the safety of what we consume. Regarding voting, blockchain could revolutionize the process by making it safe and tamper-proof, ensuring that every vote is counted accurately, and strengthening our democracy.

As we explore cryptocurrencies and blockchain, it's important to remember the responsibilities that come with this new technology. Cryptocurrencies could be a game-changer for people who don't have access to traditional banking, offering a more inclusive financial system where everyone has the chance to succeed.

Let's celebrate the progress we're making—whether it's adopting eco-friendly mining practices or using blockchain to support important causes. Each step forward reminds us that technology can be a force for good.

In this journey, we're exploring new digital frontiers and ensuring we do it responsibly and with integrity. By pushing the boundaries of what's possible with cryptocurrencies and blockchain while staying true to our values, we're building a prosperous future where technology serves the economy and society in meaningful ways. So, get excited about the possibilities, but stay grounded in the principles that guide us. Together, we can make this new digital world a better place for everyone.

## 2.6 Interactive Element: Deciphering the Code - A Cryptocurrency Quiz

In the realm of digital finance, where the allure of cryptocurrencies and their promise of a decentralized future is strong, the pursuit of knowledge is as crucial as the quest for wealth. This quiz, designed to test and enhance your understanding, is a crucible that challenges you to delve into the depths of your knowledge, question, and reason. It invites you to emerge with a sharpened perspective on digital currencies and the technology that powers them.

### Question 1: The Genesis Block

Which cryptocurrency's creation is marked by the mining of its "genesis block," a term that signifies the birth of this digital asset?

A) Ethereum

B) Bitcoin

C) Ripple

D) Litecoin

The genesis block, often shrouded in a veil of digital lore, is the cornerstone of a cryptocurrency's blockchain. It is the alpha, the origin from which all subsequent blocks derive their lineage, each carrying forward the cryptographic legacy inscribed in this primordial block.

*Answer: B) Bitcoin.* Bitcoin is a type of digital money that allows people to send and receive payments without needing a bank or middleman. Its purpose is to give individuals more control over their money, offering a faster and often cheaper way to make transactions, especially across countries. The value of Bitcoin comes from its limited supply—only 21 million will ever exist—and the trust people have in its system. It's decentralized, meaning no single person or government controls it, so some people see it as "digital gold" and a way to protect their money from inflation or unstable financial systems.

## Question 2: The Enigmatic Inventor

The identity of Bitcoin's creator remains one of the digital age's most compelling mysteries. Under what pseudonym did this person or group of individuals introduce themselves?

A) Vitalik Buterin

B) Satoshi Nakamoto

C) Dan Larimer

D) Charlie Lee

In the annals of digital finance, few figures loom as large or as enigmatic as Bitcoin's architect. This pseudonym, a cipher unto itself, encapsulates the ethos of anonymity and decentralization that defines the cryptocurrency realm.

*Answer: B) Satoshi Nakamoto.* Satoshi Nakamoto is the mysterious name used by the person (or group of people) who created Bitcoin, the first and most famous cryptocurrency. In 2008, Satoshi published a paper that explained how Bitcoin would work as a new kind of digital money, completely decentralized, meaning no banks or governments control it. They also built the first version of Bitcoin's software and mined the first Bitcoins. Interestingly, no one knows who Satoshi Nakamoto really is—their identity remains a secret, adding a lot of mystery to the story of Bitcoin's origin. Today, Bitcoin is the most valuable cryptocurrency making the mystery of its creator even more intriguing!

### Question 3: A Ledger Unbound

Blockchain technology underpins cryptocurrencies, but its applications transcend digital currencies. Which of the following is NOT a real-world application of blockchain technology?

A) Voting systems
B) Supply chain management
C) Energy consumption monitoring
D) Time travel

As the foundational fabric of cryptocurrencies, blockchain's potential unfurls across a spectrum of uses, each leveraging its transparency, security, and immutability. Yet, among the myriad applications, some realms remain beyond blockchain's reach. Understanding these applications is key to mastering the digital finance landscape.

*Answer: D) Time travel.* Only in our dreams, right?!

## Question 4: The Mechanism of Consensus

Proof of Work (PoW) and Proof of Stake (PoS) represent two distinct consensus mechanisms within blockchain technology. Which of these is renowned for its energy efficiency?

A) Proof of Work
B) Proof of Stake
C) Both equally
D) Neither

In the quest for consensus, where the collective's veracity of transactions must be upheld, these mechanisms are guardians of integrity. Yet, as stewards of blockchain, their approaches to achieving consensus diverge, each with energy consumption and efficiency implications.

*Answer: B) Proof of Stake.* Proof of Stake (PoS) is a fair method of determining who can validate transactions and add new blocks to a blockchain, all without the excessive energy consumption of older systems. In PoS, instead of deploying numerous computers to solve intricate problems (as in Proof of Work), individuals who own some cryptocurrency can 'stake' their coins to participate. This process is akin to entering a raffle—those with more coins staked have a higher chance of being chosen to validate transactions, but it's still a random and equitable process. The most exciting aspect? It's significantly more energy-efficient and eco-friendly, heralding a promising future for digital currencies!

## Question 5: The Altcoin Surge

Many alternative cryptocurrencies, or "altcoins," have emerged following Bitcoin's pioneering path. Which cryptocurrency is recognized for its focus on scalability, sustainability, and a research-driven approach to improving transaction speeds and efficiency?

A) Dogecoin
B) Ethereum
C) Litecoin
D) Cardano

In the evolving landscape of cryptocurrencies, some altcoins distinguish themselves by prioritizing innovation and sustainability. Among them, one stands out for its methodical, research-based approach to creating a more scalable and efficient blockchain system.

*Answer: D) Cardano.* Cardano is a blockchain platform that emphasizes integrity, transparency, and sustainability in the digital age, making it a vital part of addressing the growing need for trust in modern systems. In the past, Cardano distinguished itself by not just focusing on scientific research and peer-reviewed development, but by ensuring its technology is built on the strongest academic foundations. Today, Cardano is a leader in providing secure and decentralized applications, particularly in sectors like finance and identity verification, offering solutions to outdated systems lacking transparency. Looking to the future, Cardano's potential to revolutionize voting is particularly impactful. Its blockchain can provide a secure, tamper-proof method for recording votes, which could modernize and safeguard America's outdated voting systems. By ensuring every vote is accurately counted and stored with complete transparency, Cardano brings integrity and trust back into critical civic processes, contributing to a more honest and reliable culture.

**Question 6: The Digital Safe**

Cryptocurrency wallets offer sanctuary for digital assets, but their forms vary. Which type of wallet is celebrated for its robust security, akin to a digital Fort Knox?

A) Software wallets

B) Paper wallets

C) Hardware wallets

D) Online wallets

In the digital realm, where asset security becomes paramount, these wallets are bastions of protection. One type emerges as a stronghold, a bulwark against the ceaseless tide of cyber threats.

*Answer: C) Hardware wallets.* A hardware wallet is like a super-secure vault for your digital money, such as cryptocurrencies. It's a physical device that stores your private keys, like the secret passwords needed to access and manage your digital assets. The main reason it's important is because, unlike storing money on your phone or computer, a hardware wallet keeps your keys offline, making it nearly impossible for hackers to steal them. This provides a sense of security and peace of mind for teenagers interested in investing or using digital currency, as it ensures their money is protected as they build their financial future.

**Question 7: The Double-Edged Sword of Volatility**

Cryptocurrency markets are renowned for their volatility, which can spawn both opportunity and peril. What factor predominantly contributes to this volatility?

A) The unchangeable supply of most cryptocurrencies

B) Governmental regulation and oversight

C) The decentralized nature of cryptocurrencies

D) Celebrity endorsements and social media

Within the tumultuous seas of cryptocurrency markets, volatility lurks as both specter and siren, drawn forth by intrinsic and extrinsic forces to the digital currency ecosystem.

*Answer: C) The decentralized nature of cryptocurrencies.* Cryptocurrencies are decentralized, which means no single person, company, or government controls them. Instead of being managed by a central bank (like regular money), cryptocurrencies rely on a network of computers worldwide that work together to verify and record transactions. This setup makes them more secure and, importantly, transparent. Everyone can see the transactions, and no one can secretly change the system. Teenagers don't have to rely on banks or other middlemen to send, receive, or store their money—they have complete control over their digital assets.

## Question 8: The Blockchain Visionary

One individual has become synonymous with groundbreaking advancements in blockchain technology, having been a mastermind behind both Ethereum and Cardano. He is also known for his ongoing advocacy for pro-crypto regulation in the United States. Who is this influential figure?

A) Vitalik Buterin

B) Gavin Wood

C) Charles Hoskinson

D) Joseph Lubin

In the realm of blockchain innovation, few figures have had as profound an impact as this visionary. Not only did he play a key role in shaping Ethereum, the platform that revolutionized the industry with the introduction of smart contracts, but he also founded Cardano—a project that stands out for its rigorous, research-driven approach and focus on long-term scalability and sustainability. Cardano isn't just another cryptocurrency; it's a groundbreaking platform designed to solve the critical issues facing blockchain technology today, such as energy efficiency, inter-operability, and regulatory compliance. His dedication goes beyond technological advancements, as he tirelessly advocates for clear and supportive regulations in the U.S. to foster the growth and adop-tion of the crypto industry. By championing responsible innovation and pushing for a regulatory framework that balances security with opportunity, he is paving the way for a more robust and inclusive digital future.

*Answer: C) Charles Hoskinson*

This quiz is like an adventure into the world of cryptography, chal-lenging you to think and explore. Each question is a piece of the giant puzzle of digital finance, helping you uncover the mysteries of cryptocurrencies and blockchain. As you go through it, let your curiosity lead the way, guiding you through this maze of knowl-edge and bringing you closer to understanding the digital curren-cies that are set to change the future of money. Be prepared, this quiz is designed to be challenging, but it's also a great opportunity to learn and grow.

## 2.7 Overview & Final Thoughts About this Chapter

The following reflects our journey exploring digital currencies and blockchain technology. This expedition has allowed us to under-stand the complex and intricate landscapes shaped by the forces of these technologies. The journey has revealed the profound trans-formations that digital currencies are scripting in the financial universe, beginning with the genesis of Bitcoin and ending with the ethical and societal shifts engendered by this digital revolution.

The expedition commenced by exploring the essence of cryptocurrencies and how they differ from traditional monetary systems. We then delved deeper into the mechanics of blockchain technology, which underpins the decentralized ethos of digital currencies. We also discussed the potential of blockchain technology to redefine global supply chains, secure voting mechanisms, and foster transparency across numerous sectors.

As the journey progressed, we explored investment strategies and security measures required to navigate the volatile waters of cryptocurrency markets. We learned the importance of due diligence and vigilant guardianship of our digital assets. The expedition also led us to contemplate the ethical and societal implications of cryptocurrencies and blockchain, engaging with the environmental impacts of mining operations and the transformative potential of these technologies.

This journey has been rich in insights and complexities, inviting us to reflect on the transformative power of digital currencies and blockchain technology. It encourages us to reevaluate traditional financial paradigms, embrace innovation, and remain cognizant of the attendant risks and ethical considerations.

As we stand at the threshold of yet another horizon, the expedition beckons us to expand our gaze beyond the digital frontiers to the vast expanse of the global economy. The expedition prepares to weave through the dynamics of international markets, exploring the forces that animate them and the strategies informed investors employ to navigate these waters to their advantage.

In this journey of discovery, the knowledge gained from exploring digital currencies becomes the foundation for building our understanding of the broader financial world. It arms us with the insights and tools needed to navigate the complexities of the global economy, refining our investment strategies with a deeper appreciation of the forces that shape these vast markets.

With a treasure trove of digital currency and blockchain knowledge now firmly in hand, we are poised to venture into new and exciting realms. The road ahead invites us to apply the wisdom from our cryptographic exploration to the intricate world of international economics. As we navigate these uncharted waters, this adventure becomes a testament to our unwavering quest for financial mastery and the relentless pursuit of growth. The journey is far from over— it's just beginning, and the possibilities are boundless.

# CHAPTER 3
# NAVIGATING THE GLOBAL ECONOMY:
## INTERNATIONAL MARKETS

I magine a butterfly in the Amazon rainforest, its wings barely causing a stir in the dense, moist air. Yet, according to chaos theory, the flap of its wings could set off a tornado in Texas. This interconnectedness, fascinating in the natural world, parallels the global economy. A financial decision in one part of the world can send ripples across continents, affecting markets, currencies, and investments in far-flung regions. This intricate web of connections underscores the importance of broadening one's investment horizon to include international markets.

In this exploration, we dissect the allure of international investing, offering insights into why venturing beyond domestic boundaries can be a wise strategy for portfolio diversification and growth. With their varied economic cycles, the world's financial markets provide a rich tapestry of opportunities for the astute investor willing to navigate their complexities.

## 3.1 Global Investment Basics

International investing opens up a whole new world of possibilities for your portfolio. The idea is to spread your investments across different countries, reducing the risk of being too dependent on any country's economic ups and downs. Diversifying globally can help you avoid significant losses by balancing out market fluctuations in different regions.

But diversification is not just about protection—it's about tapping into rapidly growing markets with immense potential. Emerging economies, such as those in Asia or Africa, often outpace established ones in terms of growth, offering you the opportunity to be part of promising new ventures. These markets are fueled by youthful populations, rapid tech adoption, and a burgeoning middle class, making them a fertile ground for investments that could soar in value over time.

Investing internationally also adds another layer of excitement: currency diversification. By holding assets in various currencies, you can protect yourself against the decline of any single currency and even boost your returns if exchange rates move in your favor.

Embarking on your international investing journey is more manageable than it may seem. Understanding global market trends and currency risks is crucial, but there are simple ways to do this. One such way is investing in international ETFs (Exchange-Traded Funds) or mutual funds. These funds allow you to invest in multiple countries and sectors simultaneously, making global investment straightforward and cost-effective. Whether tracking a foreign market index or investing in an actively managed fund, these options provide a passport to the worldwide stage with just a few clicks.

For those who want to dive deeper, American Depository Receipts (ADRs) and foreign ordinaries are your gateway to directly owning shares in international companies. ADRs let you buy shares of foreign companies on U.S. stock exchanges, making it super easy to add some international flavor to your portfolio without needing to navigate the complexities of foreign trading. If you're feeling adventurous, you can even trade shares directly on global exchanges, immersing yourself in the action abroad.

Sure, investing internationally can be a bit more complex, but that's part of what makes it exciting! With the proper knowledge and tools, you can explore new markets, seize opportunities world-wide, and build a diversified portfolio ready to take on whatever the global economy throws. It's not just about growing your wealth—it's about experiencing the thrill of worldwide investing and watching your money work for you worldwide.

**Visual Element: Chart of Global Market Trends**

A comprehensive chart visualizing global market trends over the last decade can elucidate the fluctuations and growth patterns across different regions. This visual guide underscores the cyclical nature of economic expansions and contractions, highlighting the periods of significant growth in emerging markets compared to developed ones. Such a chart not only serves as an educational tool but can also aid investors in identifying historical trends and potential future opportunities in international investing.

**Choosing International Stocks: A Checklist**

- Research Market Trends: Analyze the target market's economic indicators, political stability, and growth prospects.

- Evaluate Currency Risks: Consider the potential impact of currency fluctuations on investment returns.
- Assess Regulatory Environment: Understand the regulatory framework governing investments in the target market.
- Diversify Across Regions and Sectors: Spread investments to mitigate risks associated with specific regions or sectors.
- Monitor Global Economic Indicators: Keep abreast of global economic developments that could affect international markets.

In delving into international markets, investors unlock possibilities that transcend the confines of domestic investments. This foray into the global economy not only diversifies one's portfolio but also enriches the investor's understanding of the interconnectedness of world markets. Through meticulous research, strategic planning, and a keen eye for opportunity, navigating the complexities of international investing can yield substantial rewards, positioning the investor for robust financial growth in the global arena.

## 3.2 Understanding Economic Indicators

In the realm of global finance, where nations' economies interlace in a complex ballet of influences and outcomes, the role of economic indicators cannot be overstated. These indicators, the pulse points of financial health, serve as beacons, guiding investors through the fog of market speculation toward informed decision-making. Within this intricate dance, three indicators – leading, lagging, and coincident – form the choreography investors must interpret to anticipate market movements, confirm ongoing trends, or gauge the current economic landscape.

Similar to the forecast of an impending storm, leading indicators offer previews of the future economic climate. Their predictive nature lies in their ability to signal shifts in economic cycles ahead of observable changes in the market. Consider the example of stock market returns, a leading indicator often presages broader economic trends. An upward trajectory in stock prices may hint at the forthcoming economic expansion, prompting investors to adjust their portfolios in anticipation of growth. Conversely, a downturn could signal an approaching recession, urging a strategic retreat to more secure assets.

Lagging indicators, on the other hand, act as historians of the financial world, confirming trends after they have been established. Unemployment rates exemplify this category, reflecting economic health only after changes have permeated the job market. Another critical lagging indicator is the workforce participation rate, which measures the percentage of the working-age population that is either employed or actively seeking employment. This rate is significant because it provides insights into the overall health of the labor market and reveals broader economic trends, such as shifts in demographics or changes in financial confidence. For investors, these indicators, while not predictive, provide a rearview mirror perspective, affirming whether the economic path they have charted aligns with the unfolding reality. This retrospective view ensures that investment strategies, forged in anticipation of financial shifts, are grounded in actual outcomes, allowing for course corrections as necessary.

Coincident indicators, the third strand in this triad, capture the economic moment, offering a snapshot of the current state of affairs. Gross Domestic Product (GDP) growth rates exemplify this category, mirroring the economy's health in real-time. These indicators are compasses for those navigating the global investment landscape, orienting strategies to the prevailing economic conditions. A robust GDP growth rate might embolden investors to pursue aggressive expansion strategies. At the same time, a contraction could necessitate a defensive posture, prioritizing asset preservation overgrowth.

Imagine the world of finance as a massive video game, where different levels of economic indicators give you clues on how to navigate the game and win big. Each type of indicator—leading, lagging, and coincident—plays a unique role, like different power-ups that can help you anticipate what's coming next, confirm what just happened, or understand what's happening right now. But just like in any game, the usefulness of these power-ups depends on how reliable they are. The data behind these indicators comes from government agencies and non-profits, who work hard to get it right. However, sometimes there are glitches or delays, which can mess with your strategy. That's why it's essential to critically evaluate this information and combine insights from multiple sources to get a clear picture of the economic landscape.

These indicators aren't just numbers—they can significantly impact markets. Leading indicators are like a sneak peek at the next level, influencing investors' feelings and sometimes causing big market moves as people try to get ahead of the curve. Lagging indicators, on the other hand, are more like the game stats that confirm if your strategy was on point after the fact. Coincident indicators are your real-time scoreboard, giving you instant feedback on the current state of the economy and helping you make quick decisions. Together, these indicators create a roadmap that guides investors through the twists and turns of the global market.

Understanding how to use these indicators is like mastering the game. It's not enough to skim the surface—you need to dive deep into the story behind the numbers, explore how they've played out in the past, and think about what they mean for the future. This isn't just a local game either... it's global! Meaning, you must keep an eye on what's happening in other countries. A slowdown in one part of the world can send shockwaves through the global economy, affecting your investments in ways you might not expect. A wide-angle view of international economic indicators is critical to a winning investment strategy.

But don't worry, you're not playing this game alone. There are tons of resources—from government reports & expert analyses to robo-advisors—that can help you make sense of the global economic landscape. If you use them wisely, these resources can guide you to the next ample opportunity or help you avoid potential pitfalls.

With a solid grasp of economic indicators, you can confidently navigate the global market. This knowledge is like your ultimate game guide, helping you make intelligent decisions and position your investments to benefit from the ups and downs of the economic cycles. In the epic adventure of global finance, where fortunes can rise and fall on the waves of economic change, understanding these indicators isn't just helpful—it's a crucial necessity to winning the game.

## 3.3 Interactive Element: Deciphering Global Dynamics - An Investment Quiz

In the thrilling world of global finance, where the rise and fall of currencies can ripple across continents, the true superpower of an investor is the ability to anticipate and adapt quickly. It's not just about watching the news; it's about diving into the complex dance of geopolitics, market trends, and economic signals. This quiz is your chance to test your skills and sharpen your ability to make intelligent investment decisions. Remember, understanding the global markets is the key to turning knowledge into success.

**Scenario 1: The Ripple of Trade Agreements**

Imagine two major countries signing a trade deal to reduce tariffs and boost trade. This isn't just a big deal for them—it's going to shake up markets all over the world.

Question: How might this agreement impact emerging markets?

*Answer: Emerging markets might benefit from increased demand for their exports or face more competition from the major countries involved.*

Question: Which sectors are most likely to benefit in the short term?

*Answer: Sectors like technology and manufacturing could see an immediate boost due to increased trade and lowered tariffs.*

Question: As an investor, would you increase your stake in technology stocks, agricultural commodities, or manufacturing shares?

*Answer: Investing in technology and manufacturing shares might be the best move to capitalize on the trade deal.*

**Scenario 2: The Shadow of Economic Sanctions**

A group of countries just slapped economic sanctions on a nation that plays a vital role in the global supply of natural resources. The world is watching—and markets are reacting.

Question: What immediate effects might these sanctions have on the global oil price?

*Answer: The global oil price could spike due to reduced supply from the sanctioned country.*

Question: Considering the geopolitical tension, which investment strategy could safeguard your portfolio?

*Answer: Shifting investments into more stable sectors like utilities or health-care might protect your portfolio from volatility.*

Question: Would you consider reallocating investments into more stable sectors like utilities or healthcare or looking for opportunities within the volatility?

*Answer: Investing in stable sectors could be a safer bet, but those who thrive on risk might look for market volatility opportunities.*

## Scenario 3: The Surge of Inflation

Inflation is suddenly surging in a significant economy, and central banks are scrambling to react. Investors everywhere are trying to figure out what this means for their money.

Question: How does this spike in inflation influence emerging market currencies?

*Answer: Emerging market currencies might weaken as investors flock to stronger currencies or fluctuate depending on their inflation rates.*

Question: Would bonds or stocks offer a safer harbor for your investments in this scenario?

*Answer: Bonds are typically considered safer during inflation, but some stocks—especially in defensive sectors—could offer protection.*

Question: Given the historical context of inflation's impact on property values, is this an opportune moment to explore real estate investments?

*Answer: Real estate might be a wise investment during inflation as property values often increase with living costs.*

**Scenario 4: The Winds of Political Change**

A recent election in a highly regulated country has brought a pro-business leader into power. They're promising significant changes that could shake up the market.

Question: Which industries stand to gain from a loosening of regulatory constraints?

*Answer: Industries like finance, energy, and tech might grow as regulations are rolled back.*

Question: Is the potential deregulation an indicator to bolster investments in this country's market, or does the political volatility suggest caution?

*Answer: While there's potential for gains, the political volatility might suggest a cautious approach until the new policies are implemented.*

Question: Would you diversify your portfolio to include more shares from this region or wait and see to gauge the new administration's effectiveness?

*Answer: Diversifying gradually could be wise, balancing the potential for growth with the risk of political instability.*

**Scenario 5: The Breakthrough in Renewable Energy**

A company in a small market just made a massive breakthrough in renewable energy technology. This could change everything in the energy world.

Question: How might this technological advancement impact investments in traditional energy sectors?

*Answer: Traditional energy stocks might take a hit as investors shift focus to renewables, anticipating a future decrease in demand for fossil fuels.*

Question: Is this an opportune moment to increase your exposure to renewable energy stocks, or would the nascent state of the technology advise a more cautious approach?

*Answer: It could be a great time to invest in renewables, but caution is advised as the technology is still new, and the market may be volatile.*

Question: Considering the potential for global adoption, would emerging markets benefit from this innovation, and how would you adjust your investment strategy to capitalize on this trend?

*Answer: Emerging markets, especially those with abundant renewable resources, could benefit significantly. Adjusting your strategy to include these markets could be a smart move.*

## Scenario 6: The Tumult of Currency Fluctuation

A significant currency has just taken a nosedive, sending shockwaves through the global economy. This affects everything from trade balances to debt payments.

Question: What immediate steps would you take to mitigate the impact of this devaluation on your international investments?

*Answer: Hedging with commodities or reallocating into more stable currencies could mitigate the impact.*

Question: Given this currency fluctuation, would commodities or futures present a viable hedging strategy?

*Answer: Commodities and futures are often used to hedge against currency fluctuations.*

Question: How would you reassess your portfolio's geographical distribution to weather the potential long-term effects of this devaluation?

*Answer: Diversifying into regions less affected by the currency devaluation could help stabilize your portfolio.*

This quiz isn't just about answering questions—it's about stepping into the shoes of an investor navigating the high-stakes world of global finance. Each scenario challenges you to think critically, make tough decisions, and see the bigger picture. As you explore these situations, remember: the more you understand the global markets, the better you'll be to turn knowledge into success. In conclusion, mastering the art of predicting and adapting to global events can sharpen your ability to make intelligent investment decisions in the thrilling world of international finance.

## 3.4 The Impact of Technology on Global Markets

In our examination of international markets, it is crucial to acknowledge the profound impact of technology on the global economy. Technology has fundamentally altered how we access and interact with markets and has significantly influenced international trade, finance, and investment dynamics.

### Globalization and Market Access

Technology has hastened globalization, breaking down barriers and enabling businesses and investors to operate internationally. High-speed internet, advanced telecommunications, and digital platforms have made it easier than ever for investors to access global markets. This increased access has led to greater market efficiency and liquidity, as more participants worldwide can engage in trading and investment activities.

Online trading platforms like Interactive Brokers and TD Ameritrade allow investors to buy and sell securities on international exchanges with just a few clicks. This accessibility means that investors are no longer limited to their domestic markets and can swiftly diversify their portfolios by investing in foreign assets.

## Real-Time Data and Decision-Making

The availability of real-time data has transformed how investors analyze and respond to market conditions. Various factors influence global financial markets, including geopolitical events, economic indicators, and currency fluctuations. With technology, investors can monitor these developments in real-time, allowing them to make more informed decisions quickly. News aggregators and financial apps like Bloomberg, The Wall Street Journal, Reuters, and the Economist provide up-to-the-minute information on global markets, helping investors stay informed about the latest trends and events that could impact their international investments.

## The Role of Algorithmic Trading

Algorithmic trading, which uses computer programs to execute trades based on predefined criteria, has become increasingly prevalent in global markets. This technology allows for high-frequency trading and can manage large volumes of trades in milliseconds, significantly impacting market dynamics. While algorithmic trading can increase market efficiency, it can also contribute to volatility, particularly in international markets where different time zones and regulatory environments come into play. Many large financial institutions use algorithmic trading to capitalize on minor price discrepancies between various markets, known as arbitrage. This can lead to rapid changes in asset prices, creating opportunities and risks for investors in international markets.

## The Digitalization of Currency

The rise of digital currencies and blockchain technology is another critical development in the global economy. Cryptocurrencies like Bitcoin, Ethereum, and Cardano have introduced new forms of cross-border transactions, bypassing traditional banking systems and potentially reducing the costs and complexities associated with international trade. While still in their early stages, these technologies have the potential to reshape how global markets function. The adoption of digital currencies for international transactions is growing, with some companies and countries exploring blockchain for trade finance, reducing the time and costs associated with cross-border payments.

The influence of technology on the global economy, particularly international markets, cannot be overstated. As technology continues to evolve, it will undoubtedly bring new opportunities and challenges for investors. Understanding how to leverage these technological advancements will be crucial for navigating the complexities of global investing in the years to come.

## 3.5 Overview & Final Thoughts About this Chapter

In this chapter, we explored the vast and complex world of the global economy, from local markets to the bustling hub of international finance. Our journey has revealed that the worldwide market is not a single entity but a diverse collection of individual markets, each with its own economic indicators, political climates, and market dynamics.

We have delved into the intricacies of investing abroad and emphasized the importance of diversification in building a robust investment portfolio. By spreading investments across different markets, sectors, and currencies, investors can protect themselves against the volatility of any one economy while leveraging global economic trends and reducing risk.

Moreover, we have discussed economic indicators, essential signals that help investors navigate market uncertainties. Understanding these indicators allows investors to predict market changes and align their investments with upcoming trends based on solid data and analysis rather than guesswork.

We have included an interactive investment scenarios quiz to bring theory to life. This quiz challenges readers to apply what they've learned in real-world situations, blending theoretical knowledge with practical application. This tool is an excellent way for investors to sharpen their decision-making skills in a controlled, risk-free environment.

In summary, while investing in international markets can be complex and challenging, it offers unique opportunities for growth and diversification that are not available through domestic investments alone. Informed investors, equipped with knowledge of economic indicators and a diversification strategy, are well-prepared to navigate these complexities confidently.

This chapter is just the beginning of a broader exploration into finance. It sets the stage for a deeper discussion on ethical finance and socially responsible investing, which explores how financial returns can be balanced with positive contributions to the world. This chapter invites investors to consider not only the profitability of their portfolios but also their impact on environmental sustainability, social justice, and corporate governance.

The principles of diversification and strategic planning discussed in international investing also apply to ESG investing, helping investors choose assets that reflect their financial goals and values. This narrative encourages investors to view finance as a force for the good in our world and integrate ethical considerations into our investment strategies, enhancing the financial journey with a sense of purpose and responsibility. You're stepping into a world where finance isn't just about making money—it's about making a difference. By learning how to invest wisely and ethically, you're setting yourself up for success and contributing to a better, more responsible world. Keep exploring, and remember, your financial journey can be a powerful tool for positive change!

## SHARE YOUR LIGHT TO INSPIRE OTHERS

**"Your review can light up someone's world."** Like Steve Jobs, who forged his own path, you can do something extraordinary today. Did you know that selfless acts of kindness make you happier and more fulfilled? This journey is about sparking change together. Will you help someone by sharing your thoughts on this book? They're full of dreams, just like you. Every review helps guide them to success. It takes less than a minute and costs nothing—but could change a life! To leave your review, **scan the QR code below.**

If helping an unseen friend warms your heart, you're our hero. Welcome to the family. You're one of us now.

A million thanks from the core of my heart. Let's dive back into the adventure that awaits us.

**Your biggest cheerleader, Chad**

# CHAPTER 4

# THE SUSTAINABLE TREASURE MAP:

## SOCIALLY RESPONSIBLE AND ESG INVESTING

Socially responsible investing (SRI) and Environmental, Social, and Governance (ESG) criteria are the future of finance. These investment strategies align financial goals with ethical values and help positively impact the world. With the sustainable investment market now over $30 trillion, it is clear that more investors are realizing the power of these principles.

By choosing SRI, you can make investment choices that align with your personal values while still achieving financial returns. This approach reflects changing societal values, where investors want to drive progress and equality. SRI covers a range of strategies, from community investing to excluding industries that conflict with one's ethical stance.

ESG investing evaluates companies based on environmental, social, and governance practices. This framework helps investors make decisions that reflect their values and emphasizes the importance of corporate responsibility in areas such as environmental change, labor practices, and ethical leadership. The growing demand for ESG-focused products is evident in the proliferation of mutual funds, brokerage firms, and robo-advisors offering these investment options.

Investing in socially responsible companies, such as Patagonia and IKEA, is a wise financial decision and a way to positively impact the environment and society. These companies demonstrate how capital can act as a catalyst for environmental innovation and social progress. Patagonia is known for its commitment to sustainability and environmental activism, while IKEA focuses on eco-friendly materials and energy efficiency. The infusion of capital into responsible entities fosters a cycle of positive development that benefits society at large. By choosing SRI (Socially Responsible Investing) and ESG (Environmental, Social, and Governance) investing, you can make a difference in the world while securing your financial future.

## 4.1 Top 3 Visible Benefits of ESG Investing

ESG investing has been proven to create visible environmental, societal, and long-term benefits. By directing capital towards companies prioritizing sustainability, ESG investing encourages advancements in green technology, leading to reductions in carbon footprints. It also promotes social justice, fair labor practices, and community engagement, creating more equitable societies. The focus on governance within the ESG framework fosters transparency, accountability, and ethical leadership within companies, which mitigates risks and contributes to the long-term stability and performance of investments.

To implement the principles outlined in this chapter, readers can engage in a highly effective and interactive exercise that aligns their investment choices with their values. The exercise includes identifying core values, researching and evaluating potential investments using ESG ratings and sustainability reports, building a diversified portfolio that reflects their values, and regularly reviewing and adjusting their portfolio to accommodate evolving priorities and market conditions. By following these steps, investors can confidently invest their money in a way that aligns with their values and contributes to a more sustainable and equitable future.

By bridging the gap between theory and practice, this exercise empowers investors to make informed decisions that resonate with their ethical convictions, fostering a sense of fulfillment that transcends financial gains.

In this era, where the threads of finance, environmental stewardship, and social progress intertwine more tightly than ever, the principles of SRI and ESG investing offer a map for navigating the complex landscape of modern investment. By adopting these frameworks, investors can realize financial returns and contribute to constructing a sustainable, equitable future. In exploring the foundations and impacts of SRI and ESG investing, this chapter illuminates the path for investors seeking to align their financial endeavors with their values, charting a course toward a more responsible and impactful form of investment.

## 4.2 Evaluating ESG Investments

Investing can feel like solving a complicated puzzle, especially when you want to do it ethically. It's like finding your way through a maze, where the goal is to uncover sustainable wealth that aligns with your values. To get there, diving into ESG (Environmental, Social, and Governance) principles is empowering, as it equips you with the knowledge to make informed and ethical investment decisions.

One way to navigate this maze is to use negative and positive screening. Negative screening involves excluding companies that don't match your ethical standards, such as those involved in tobacco or fossil fuels. On the other hand, positive screening focuses on companies that champion sustainability, social responsibility, and good governance, thereby aligning your investments with your values.

You can also try something called portfolio tilt. This method gives more weight to companies that excel in ESG practices, ensuring your investments align with your values and tap into the growing sustainability trend. Taking it a step further, ESG integration means weaving ESG principles into every part of the investment process, ensuring your entire portfolio reflects your ethical stance.

Plenty of tools are available to help you find suitable ESG investments, providing reassurance. Resources like the USSIF Sustainable Investment Mutual Funds and ETFs Chart, Sustainalytics ESG Ratings, and the MSCI ESG Ratings & Climate Search Tool offer valuable data and insights. For example, the Charles Schwab SRI Screen filters investment options through a socially responsible lens. At the same time, the Refinitiv ESG Scores clearly show how well companies stick to ESG principles, giving you the confidence to make secure and ethical investment choices.

## Understanding ESG Scores

If you're serious about socially responsible investing, ESG scores are a vital tool to consider. These scores, provided by rating agencies, tell you how companies and funds perform regarding their environmental impact, social contributions, and governance integrity. They are not just random numbers but a comprehensive analysis of each company's performance across various ESG criteria based on a deep dive into publicly available data, reports, and disclosures.

High ESG scores signal more than good business—they show a company's commitment to sustainable practices and ethical operations. Companies with top ESG scores demonstrate that they're serious about their responsibilities to the environment and society, and they're actively working on initiatives that contribute to a sustainable future. By aligning their operations with broader societal goals, these companies inspire investors who care about making a positive impact and offer the potential for financial growth. So, if you're looking to make investments that matter, keep an eye out for companies with high ESG scores—they're leading the charge toward a better future and can inspire you to make a positive impact while growing your wealth.

**Case Studies: Champions of ESG Investing**

Checking out companies doing well in ESG practices, such as those with high scores in environmental protection, social responsibility, and corporate governance, shows that being ethical and making money can go hand in hand. Unilever is an excellent example of this. They are deeply committed to sustainability and have set ambitious goals, like achieving net-zero emissions across their value chain by 2039. By reducing its carbon footprint and improving energy efficiency, Unilever is boosting its financial performance and earning higher ESG scores.

Vital Capital, another company making strides in ESG investing, has directed its investments towards sub-Saharan Africa. Their projects, which focus on enhancing people's lives through infrastructure development, renewable energy utilization, and healthcare provision, have not only benefited society and the environment but also yielded returns for investors. Similarly, companies like Patagonia, renowned for their sustainable business practices, and Ørsted, a leader in renewable energy, are inspiring examples of successful ESG investing.

These examples serve as a powerful reminder that ESG investing is indeed a win-win strategy. It not only leads to better financial performance but also ensures positive social and environmental outcomes. In this future, success is measured not just by monetary gains but by the tangible difference made in the world. This dual benefit should instill confidence and optimism in investors about the potential of ESG investing.

To evaluate ESG investments, you need a mix of tools, ethics, and knowledge. This includes using ESG rating agencies, conducting thorough research on a company's ESG practices, and understanding the potential risks and returns. Using these resources, investors can find suitable investments that help the environment and society while making money. This way, investors can create a portfolio reflecting their values and commitment to improving the world.

## 4.3 Getting Started with SRI and ESG Investing

Investing in socially responsible ESG (Environmental, Social, and Governance) funds may seem daunting. Still, it requires careful planning and a commitment to positively impact the world. This type of investment goes beyond a simple financial transaction. It aligns your capital with broader global sustainability and social equity goals.

The first step is to build a portfolio that balances SRI/ESG investments and traditional assets. This requires a thorough understanding of financial principles and a deep introspection of personal values and ethical standards. Taking control and finding this balance can significantly and positively impact society and achieve economic growth.

So, don't be intimidated and take that first step towards socially responsible and ESG investing, to start building your portfolio today! Remember, with the right mindset and strategic planning, you can create a financial future that aligns with your values and makes a difference in the world.

**Crafting an SRI/ESG Portfolio: Make Your Money Matter**

Building an SRI/ESG portfolio is like creating a work of art where every decision you make reflects your values and goals. It's a journey of empowerment, starting with understanding your risk tolerance—how much risk you're willing to take on—so you can shape a portfolio that helps you reach your financial dreams and aligns with what you believe in.

When choosing investments, it's all about doing your homework. Each opportunity isn't just a way to make money—it's a chance to invest in companies making a real difference in the world. Your portfolio should reflect your commitment to the environment, social issues, and ethical business practices. Think of it as your canvas where you add in companies and sectors that share your vision for a better future.

Managing your SRI/ESG portfolio is more than just watching the numbers grow. It's about staying in the loop with real-time updates and analyses so you can always know how your investments are doing and adjust your strategy as needed. Investing is a dynamic process that requires you to be flexible, constantly reassessing your choices to keep up with the ever-evolving world of ethical investing.

## Long-Term Benefits: Do Good While Doing Well

Investing in SRI/ESG isn't just about stacking cash—it's about making a positive impact. It's about finding purpose in your investments. You can navigate market ups and downs using intelligent risk management strategies and stay ahead of the curve. When you put your money into companies focusing on sustainability, you're not just making a smart financial move—you're helping shape a better world. Supporting businesses committed to ethical practices also attracts passionate and talented people who want to make a difference, leading to innovative solutions for global challenges and a brighter future.

## Busting Common Myths: The Truth About SRI/ESG Investing

There are some misconceptions about SRI/ESG investing that just aren't true. Some people think it's just a passing trend, but the shift toward sustainability and ethical business practices is here to stay. It's driven by a growing awareness of global issues and the power of investment to help solve them, making SRI/ESG investing a vital part of the future.

Another myth is that SRI/ESG investing means giving up profits, but that's false. It's about debunking misconceptions and providing reassurance. Many studies show that these investments can perform just as well, if not better, than traditional ones. Plus, they come with the bonus of positively impacting the world. So, if you want to grow your wealth while staying true to your values, SRI/ESG investing is the way to go.

**Your Journey Begins**

Embarking on the SRI/ESG investing journey is all about being thoughtful with your choices and staying committed to your ethical principles. It's a path that promises financial growth and contributes to a more sustainable and fair world. With the power of your investments, you can help build a future that reflects the values you care about.

## 4.4 Interactive Element: Crafting Your Ethical Portfolio

Building an ethical investment portfolio is more than just planning —it's about taking hands-on action to align your financial goals with your values. In this section, you'll follow these step-by-step actions to create a personalized, ethical investment strategy.

### Step 1: Identify Your Core Values and Interests

Grab a notebook or open a new document: List your core values and the causes that matter most to you. These could include climate change, fair labor practices, corporate transparency, community development, or any other issues you feel passionate about.

Reflect on each issue: Spend a few minutes thinking about why these issues are important and how they align with your beliefs. Write down your thoughts and insights, as they will guide your investment decisions.

Prioritize your values: Rank your values in order of importance. This will help you focus on the causes that resonate most deeply as you select investments.

## Step 2: Research SRI/ESG Investment Opportunities

Start with a search: Use online resources like ESG rating websites, investment platforms, and financial news outlets to research companies and funds aligning with your identified values.

Create a shortlist: As you find companies or funds that align with your values, add them to a shortlist. Include notes on how each one aligns with your values and any standout initiatives or ESG scores they have.

Dig deeper: For each company or fund on your shortlist, dig into their business practices, recent news, and financial performance. Make sure they align with your values and have a solid track record and potential for growth.

## Step 3: Match Your Values to Specific Investments

Review your shortlist: Go through your identified companies and funds and match them to your prioritized values. Ask yourself which ones best represent your beliefs and have the potential for financial returns.

Evaluate financial viability: Assess each investment's economic health and prospects. Consider factors like past performance, industry trends, and growth potential.

Make your selections: Choose the companies or funds that best align with both your values and financial goals. These are the investments you'll add to your ethical portfolio.

## Step 4: Reflect on Your Investment Choices

Answer reflective prompts: Take some time to think about the impact of your investments by answering these prompts:

How does investing in renewable energy companies contribute to your vision of a sustainable future?

In what ways do supporting funds that prioritize gender diversity advance social equity?

Reflect on how your investments promote fair labor practices. How does this align with your views on human rights?

Write down your reflections: Document your thoughts on these prompts to deepen your understanding of the connection between your financial choices and ethical beliefs.

**Step 5: Journal Your Ethical Investment Strategy**

Create a journal entry: Write a detailed account of your ethical investment journey in your notebook or document. Start with how you identified your values, then explain the research process, and finally, describe why you chose the investments you did.

Reflect on your growth: Consider how this process has influenced your perspective on investing. How has it changed your understanding of money's role in making a positive impact? This journey is not just about financial gain, but also about personal growth and reflection. It's an opportunity to deepen your understanding of the connection between your financial choices and ethical beliefs.

Keep your journal updated: As you continue investing, use this journal to track your progress, record any changes in your strategy, and reflect on how your portfolio evolves. Remember, this is an ongoing journey, and your commitment to ethical investing is a powerful force for positive change.

**Your Ethical Portfolio: A Blueprint for Impact**

By following these steps, you've not only created an ethical investment portfolio that reflects who you are and what you care about, but you've also empowered yourself. This isn't just about making money—it's about making a difference. Every investment you've chosen is a step towards building a world that aligns with your sustainability, equity, and corporate responsibility vision. Your portfolio is more than just numbers on a screen—it's a powerful tool for change, proving that financial growth and ethical progress can go hand in hand. Keep this momentum going, and let your investments be the foundation of a legacy you'll be proud to leave behind. So start your journey with confidence, knowing that you can make a real difference while securing your financial success.

## 4.5 Overview & Final Thoughts About this Chapter

In the exciting world of socially responsible and ESG (Environmental, Social, and Governance) investing, we've ventured into new territory together, uncovering opportunities that enhance your financial future and make a real impact on our planet and its people. This chapter has shown how to invest in a way that genuinely matters—where economic success aligns with ethical action and a commitment to improving the world.

By exploring SRI (Socially Responsible Investing) and ESG investing, we've developed a blueprint for evaluating investments beyond just financial returns. Investing in companies that promote renewable energy or prioritize diversity and inclusion exemplifies how you can make a difference. Successful investing isn't just about making money—it's about creating positive change and feeling a sense of accomplishment. This sense of fulfillment is a reward in itself, making your investment journey more meaningful.

Every investment decision you make is a powerful tool that can shape not only your financial future but also the world around you. Whether you choose to invest in renewable energy, companies with strong diversity policies, or real estate, your values can guide you. Your investments are a reflection of the world you want to build, and your financial choices have the power to significantly impact society and the planet, making you a significant player in this global change. This sense of empowerment is a key aspect of socially responsible and ESG investing.

Our exploration has also focused on practical strategies for starting your SRI and ESG investing journey. By aligning your values with smart financial decisions, you can achieve your goals while contributing positively to society and the environment. These are not just theoretical concepts, but actionable steps that you can take to make a tangible difference. This alignment gives you a sense of control and security, knowing that your investments are in line with your values and making a positive impact.

As we delve into real estate investing, particularly through Real Estate Investment Trusts (REITs), a type of investment that allows individuals to invest in income-producing real estate without having to buy, manage, or finance any properties, a myriad of opportunities for growth, diversification, and ethical impact unfold before us. Armed with this knowledge, you will confidently navigate the investment landscape, making deliberate choices that enhance your portfolio and contribute positively to the world around you.

# CHAPTER 5

# COMMANDING THE HIGH SEAS:

## REAL ESTATE AND REITS ADVANCED STRATEGIES

In a marketplace where the tangible intersects with the intangible, real estate is a bastion of value, a testament to the enduring allure of physical assets in an increasingly digital world. The draw of real estate as an investment vehicle lies not just in its capacity to generate passive income or appreciate over time but in its ability to offer a tangible connection to the economic fabric of communities. Amid this landscape, Real Estate Investment Trusts (REITs) emerge as a sophisticated tool, democratizing access to real estate markets and offering a bridge between the allure of real estate and the liquidity of stock markets.

The appeal of diving into real estate investments, mainly through the lens of REITs, is akin to the experience of planting a garden. Just as a gardener cultivates a patch of earth, sowing seeds that will grow, flourish, and yield over time, so too does the investor in REITs nurture a portfolio of properties. But just as a garden's success depends on the health of its soil, the foundation of your investment—careful research, due diligence, and a deep under-standing of market trends—is crucial for growth. Just as a gardener enriches the soil with nutrients and regularly manages water levels and weeds to ensure a bountiful harvest, an investor must monitor and adjust their portfolio. By nurturing this foundation, your REIT investments can provide a steady stream of dividends, much like the recurring bloom of a well-tended garden.

### 5.1 What are Real Estate Investment Trusts (REITs)?

At its core, a REIT is a company that owns, operates, or finances income-producing real estate across a range of property sectors. These include everything from apartment buildings and hospitals to cell towers and hotels. Much like mutual funds, REITs allow individuals to invest in large-scale, income-producing real estate without directly buying or managing any property. This structure simplifies investment and provides liquidity not typically associated with direct real estate investments. The shares of most REITs are traded on major stock exchanges, enabling investors to buy and sell with the ease of trading stocks.

The mechanism through which REITs operate is straightforward yet powerful. By pooling numerous investors' capital, these trusts can purchase and manage a diverse portfolio of real estate assets. The revenue generated from these properties, whether through rent, lease, or sales, is then distributed back to the investors as dividends. The requirement for REITs to distribute at least 90% of their taxable income directly correlates to the attractive dividend yields they often offer, marking them as a potent source of passive income.

### The Strategic Value of REITs in a Portfolio

The inclusion of REITs in an investment portfolio offers several strategic benefits. Primarily, they serve as a hedge against inflation.

Real estate values and rents typically increase in an inflationary environment, translating into higher dividend payouts for REIT investors. Moreover, the diversification provided by REITs is substantial. Investing in real estate across various sectors and geographical locations can mitigate risk and reduce the volatility of an investment portfolio, offering a buffer against the fluctuations of the stock market.

However, the decision to invest in REITs should be underpinned by a thorough analysis of the trust's property holdings, management quality, and dividend yield history. The performance of a REIT is intrinsically linked to the health of the real estate market and the economic sectors it encompasses. Thus, an understanding of market conditions, alongside an evaluation of the REIT's strategic direction and operational efficiency, is paramount.

**Visual Element: REITs Performance Chart**

A compelling way to grasp the potential of REITs is through a visual comparison of their performance relative to other investment vehicles over time. A chart illustrating the annualized returns of REITs against benchmarks such as the S&P 500 or bond indices over a decade provides a clear picture of their performance in various economic climates. Such a visual aids in contextualizing the role of REITs within a diversified investment strategy, highlighting their resilience and the steadiness of returns they can offer.

**Navigating the Seas of REIT Investment**

When contemplating an investment in REITs, consider the landscape as a captain would the sea. Just as currents, winds, and tides dictate the course of a voyage, so do market trends, economic indicators, and sector performance, which guide the investment in REITs. Like the seasoned sailor, the savvy investor knows when to set sail with the wind at their back, capitalizing on favorable market conditions and when to anchor, awaiting clearer skies.

A prudent approach involves a mix of equity REITs, which own and manage properties, and mortgage REITs (mREITs), which finance real estate. This blend diversifies the investment across different facets of the real estate market. It balances the income-generation potential with the growth opportunities inherent in property ownership and management.

**Interactive Element: Portfolio Diversification Exercise**

Now it's time to get hands-on and apply what you've learned about REITs by building your diversified REIT portfolio. This exercise will guide you through the process, helping you understand how to balance different sectors and geographical regions to create a robust investment strategy.

**Step 1: Set Your Investment Amount**

Start by deciding on a hypothetical investment amount. Let's say you have $100,000 to allocate across various REITs. Write down this amount as your starting point.

**Step 2: Research and Select REITs**

Use online resources or financial platforms to research different REITs. Focus on REITs that operate in various sectors, such as:

- Residential (e.g., apartment buildings)
- Healthcare (e.g., hospitals, nursing homes)
- Industrial (e.g., warehouses, distribution centers)
- Retail (e.g., shopping malls)

- Office (e.g., commercial office spaces)
- Specialty (e.g., cell towers, data centers)

As you research, pay attention to each REIT's property holdings, dividend yield, management quality, and performance history. Choose at least five different REITs that you believe have strong potential.

### Step 3: Allocate Your Funds

Now, allocate your $100,000 across the REITs you've selected. Be strategic—consider each sector's growth potential, the geographical regions they operate in, and their dividend yields. Write down how much of your hypothetical investment you put into each REIT and explain your reasoning for each choice.

For example:

$25,000 in a healthcare REIT because of its stable dividend and growth potential due to an aging population.

$20,000 in an industrial REIT focused on warehouses, given the rise of e-commerce.

### Step 4: Analyze the Diversification

Once you've allocated your funds, take a step back and analyze your portfolio. Consider the following questions:

Sector Diversity: Are you spread across different sectors to mitigate risk?

Geographical Spread: Do your REITs cover various regions to protect against local economic downturns?

Income vs. Growth: How balanced is your portfolio between REITs offering high dividends (income) and those with strong growth potential?

Adjust to ensure your portfolio is well-diversified and aligned with your investment goals.

## Step 5: Reflect and Document

Reflect on the decisions you made during this exercise. Write a portfolio summary explaining your choices and how they will perform. Consider any market trends or economic indicators that influenced your decisions.

This exercise has guided you through the practical steps of building a diversified REIT portfolio. By actively engaging in this process, you've gained a deeper understanding of how to allocate investments strategically across various sectors and regions. Remember, just as a garden flourishes with careful planning and maintenance, your REIT investments can also thrive with thoughtful management and ongoing evaluation.

## 5.2 Real Estate Investment Trusts (REITs)

REITs are the ultimate shortcut to owning real estate without the hassle. Imagine investing in everything from skyscrapers to shopping malls and even hospitals, but doing it with the ease of buying a stock. That's the power of REITs—they give you a piece of the real estate market while keeping things simple and liquid, meaning you can buy or sell your shares anytime. This simplicity should reassure you and give you the confidence to explore this investment option.

At their core, REITs pool money from many investors to buy and manage income-generating properties. The cool part? They must pay out at least 90% of their profits as dividends, making them a reliable source of income. This reliability should give you a sense of security and ease, knowing that your investment can provide a steady income.

But investing in REITs isn't just about picking the ones with the highest returns. It would be best to look deeper—check out the types of properties they own, how well those properties are managed, and the overall health of the real estate market. It's like curating a playlist: You want a mix that matches your vibe, whether it's steady income, growth potential, or a bit of both.

REITs also come with the advantage of liquidity, meaning you can easily adjust your investments as market conditions change. With options ranging from publicly traded REITs to REIT-focused mutual funds and ETFs, you can tailor your investment to fit your goals and risk tolerance. This flexibility should empower you and make you feel in control of your investment decisions.

An intelligent approach might involve blending equity REITs, which own and operate properties, with mortgage REITs (mRE-ITs), which focus on financing real estate. This mix can give you a balanced exposure to the real estate world, combining the potential for growth with a steady income.

In the end, REITs offer a unique way to tap into the real estate market without buying or managing property directly. They provide a mix of stability, income, and growth potential, making them a versatile addition to any investment portfolio. So, whether you're aiming for steady dividends or looking to diversify your investments, REITs can be a powerful tool in your financial strategy.

## 5.3 Crowdfunding Real Estate Projects

Real estate crowdfunding is a game-changer, breaking down the barriers that once kept everyday investors out of the property market. It's a digital gathering, a community where people from all walks of life can pool their money to fund real estate projects that would otherwise be out of reach. This model opens up exciting opportunities, allowing you to invest in everything from new apartment buildings to renovating historic landmarks—all while feeling connected to a more significant movement.

Crowdfunding platforms are like online marketplaces where investors meet project creators. Through these platforms, you can invest in a wide range of real estate ventures, contributing small amounts that, when combined with others, add up to the necessary funding. This approach makes real estate investing accessible to everyone, not just the wealthy.

Choosing the right platform is crucial. Like picking the right apps for your phone, you must find a platform that fits your needs and values. Look at the types of projects they offer, their past performance, fees, and how well they support and communicate with investors. Your choice of platform will shape your investment experience, so it's worth doing some homework.

While the potential for high returns is a big draw, it's important to remember that with great reward comes significant risk. Real estate projects can face delays, market changes, or even fail altogether. An intelligent investor weighs these risks against the possible rewards, staying alert to market shifts and ready to adapt. However, this potential for high returns keeps optimism alive in real estate crowdfunding.

Crowdfunding projects vary widely in their goals and timelines. You could invest in the renovation of urban housing, helping to revitalize communities while earning rental income. Or you could go for commercial developments that take longer but offer more significant returns. Your choices should reflect your financial goals and risk tolerance.

Due diligence, or investigating and understanding a potential investment, is key before committing your money to real estate crowdfunding. Dive deep into the details of the projects, check out the credibility of the people behind them, and understand the legalities involved. This careful research helps you pick financially sound projects that align with your vision for positive real estate development.

One challenge in real estate crowdfunding is liquidity—or how easily you can access your money. Unlike stocks or Real Estate Investment Trusts (REITs), your investment might be tied up for a while, depending on the project's timeline. Some platforms offer options to exit early, but these often come with restrictions. Understanding this aspect is essential for managing your overall investment strategy.

Real estate crowdfunding has opened up new possibilities. It lets you invest in the property market with others, sharing the risks and rewards. It's a way to contribute to real estate projects that transform communities and create meaningful spaces. As you explore this investment path, remember that your decisions impact more than just your wallet—they shape the world around you.

## 5.4 How to Craft a Diversified Real Estate Portfolio

Investing in real estate not only offers stability but also the potential for significant growth, which can be particularly appealing to those who want to build a solid financial foundation while exploring various avenues for returns. This section invites you to create a diversified real estate portfolio by blending REITs, direct property investments, and real estate crowdfunding. It's like putting together a puzzle where each piece represents your risk tolerance and financial goals.

## Guidelines for Balancing Your Portfolio

Creating a well-balanced real estate portfolio starts with understanding the unique benefits and risks of each investment type:

REITs (Real Estate Investment Trusts) offer high liquidity and steady dividend yields, making them a reliable and secure base for your portfolio. Direct Property Investments require more significant capital but offer potential rental income and long-term appreciation. They add a tangible asset to your portfolio.

Crowdfunding: This option is more speculative but can offer potentially high returns, making it an intriguing way to invest in specific projects with the pooled resources of other investors. The key to balancing your portfolio lies in your risk tolerance. If you prefer stability, you might allocate more to REITs. If you're comfortable with a bit more risk, you could spread your investment evenly across the three options or even lean towards crowdfunding if you seek higher potential returns.

## Interactive Exercise: Portfolio Construction

Now, let's get hands-on. Imagine you have a $10,000 budget to invest across REITs, direct property, and crowdfunding opportunities. This exercise will help you apply your knowledge by creating a personalized real estate portfolio.

### Step 1: Initial Allocation

Start by distributing your $10,000 based on your risk tolerance and financial goals:

Conservative Approach: Allocate $6,000 to REITs for steady

income, $3,000 to direct property for growth, and $1,000 to crowd-funding for small exposure to higher-risk opportunities.

Moderate Approach: Consider splitting your investment with $5,000 to REITs, $3,000 to direct property, and $2,000 to crowd-funding for a balanced mix of stability and growth potential.

Aggressive Approach: If you're seeking higher returns and can handle more risk, you might allocate $3,000 to REITs, $2,000 to direct property, and $5,000 to crowdfunding, aiming for substantial gains.

### Step 2: Adjust for Growth and Income

Reflect on your financial goals and adjust your allocations to favor growth-oriented investments (like direct property and specific crowdfunding projects) or income-generating assets (like REITs and income-focused crowdfunding).

### Step 3: Diversify by Sector and Location

Within your REIT and crowdfunding allocations, diversify further by choosing investments across different sectors (residential, commercial, healthcare) and geographic locations. This helps protect your portfolio from sector-specific and regional risks.

### Bringing It All Together

As you complete this exercise, think about why you made each decision. What factors influenced your allocation? How do your choices align with your financial goals and risk tolerance?

This portfolio construction isn't just about numbers; it's about shaping an investment strategy that reflects your vision for the future. Whether you're aiming for steady income, long-term growth, or a mix of both, this exercise is your first step in navigating the diverse world of real estate investing.

By actively engaging in this process, you're not just learning about real estate investing—you're practicing it. Your portfolio becomes a personalized strategy, crafted with analytical rigor and creative vision, designed to meet your financial objectives while resonating with your investment style.

## 5.5 Overview & Final Thoughts About this Chapter

In this chapter, we've journeyed through the exciting world of real estate and REITs, uncovering the potential and strategies behind property investment. From understanding how REITs make real estate accessible to everyone, to exploring the cutting-edge opportunities in real estate crowdfunding, we've opened the door to new ways of building wealth and making a difference in communities.

We've demystified REITs, showing how they allow you to invest in real estate markets with ease, offering liquidity and steady income. We also dove into real estate crowdfunding, revealing how it breaks down traditional barriers and lets you invest in impactful projects alongside others. This chapter wasn't just about learning —it was about taking action, with an interactive exercise that helped you craft a diversified real estate portfolio tailored to your goals.

This journey through real estate investment wasn't just about making money—it was about understanding how your investments can shape landscapes, build communities, and contribute to a better future. As we move forward, the next chapter will guide you in mastering the art of diversification, transforming your knowledge into a strategy for long-term financial success.

Advice: Remember, investing is about more than just the numbers —it's about making choices that reflect your values and goals. Stay curious, keep learning, and never be afraid to explore new opportunities. Your financial journey is just beginning!

# CHAPTER 6
# THE FINANCIAL ALCHEMIST:
## CREATING AND GROWING WEALTH THROUGH DIVERSIFICATION

In a world where certainty is as elusive as fog, the wisdom of spreading risk stands out like a lighthouse. It's akin to a seasoned gardener who plants various seeds, knowing that while some may falter, others will flourish, ensuring a bountiful harvest. This principle of diversification, a cornerstone of sound investing, transforms the investor into a financial alchemist adept at blending a spectrum of assets into a cohesive, resilient portfolio.

Imagine attending a music festival with stages scattered across the venue, each featuring a different genre. You can wander between stages, sampling classical, rock, jazz, and electronic music. This experience, rich in diversity, guarantees that regardless of your mood or preference at any moment, there's always a stage that resonates with you. Diversification in investing functions similarly, offering a mix of asset classes that cater to varying market conditions and personal financial goals.

## 6.1 Diversification Explained

Diversification is straightforward: spreading investments across multiple asset classes to mitigate risk and increase potential returns. Like a well-balanced diet that incorporates different food groups to maintain health, a diversified portfolio incorporates a variety of assets to achieve a healthy financial state. This strategy acknowledges that while investments can ebb and flow unpredictably, akin to the tides, a well-distributed portfolio can weather market volatility more smoothly.

The importance of diversification cannot be overstated, especially for young investors at the onset of their financial voyage. For them, the temptation to chase high returns from a single investment can be akin to putting all one's eggs in one basket - a risk that can lead to significant losses. Diversification serves as a safeguard, dispersing potential risks across a broader spectrum of investments, thereby reducing the impact of poor performance in any single investment on the overall portfolio health.

### Real-World Examples

Warren Buffett, often hailed as one of the greatest investors, exemplifies the power of diversification. Berkshire Hathaway's conglomerate spans multiple industries, from insurance and railroads to consumer goods and technology. This is a testament to the belief in not relying on a single sector or asset for growth. His strategy underscores a fundamental tenet of diversification: spreading investments across different assets, sectors, and geographies to tap into various sources of growth and income.

Similarly, the story of the Murugappa Group, a conglomerate that thrived on diversification, resonates deeply. Starting from a single banking venture, it expanded into a powerhouse with interests in engineering, agriculture, and finance. Their strategy of venturing into unrelated businesses ensured that a downturn in one sector wouldn't cripple the entire group, showcasing diversification's role in sustaining and growing wealth over decades.

**Visual Element: The Diversification Matrix**

A compelling way to visualize diversification is through a matrix that categorizes investments by asset class, risk level, and potential return. Like a blueprint, this matrix guides the investor in constructing a portfolio that balances high-risk, high-reward options with more stable, lower-return investments. It serves as a strategic tool, ensuring that decisions are grounded in a holistic view of the portfolio's composition.

This approach mirrors the complexity of a symphony orchestra, where diverse instruments come together under the conductor's baton to create a harmonious performance. Each instrument, or asset class, contributes its unique tone, and the blend of these sounds or investments creates the portfolio's richness.

In investing, where unpredictability is the only certainty, diversification is a beacon of strategy and foresight. It embodies the wisdom of not putting all one's financial aspirations on a singular path but instead spreading them across a landscape rich in opportunity and variation. This chapter, dedicated to unraveling the intricacies of diversification, aims to equip investors with the knowledge to navigate the financial markets confidently, crafting resilient and poised portfolios for growth.

## 6.2 Balancing a Portfolio

In the grand tapestry of investment, weaving together a portfolio that resonates with the market's rhythm and the individual's unique financial cadence emerges as a nuanced craft. This endeavor, far from merely aggregating assets, requires an astute sense of balance, a discerning eye for potential, and a steadfast commitment to asset allocation principles. At the heart of this process lies the challenge of harmonizing investments across stocks, bonds, real estate, and the broad spectrum of alternative investments, crafting a symphony of financial instruments that plays to the tune of growth, income, and security.

The orchestration of asset allocation begins with an understanding that each investment class carries its own melody of risk and reward. With their potential for robust returns, stocks dance to the beat of market volatility, offering high growth notes against economic fluctuations. Bonds, in contrast, provide a steady rhythm of fixed income, and their lower risk profile offers a counterpoint to the dynamism of stocks. Real estate, with its tangible assets and potential for rental income and capital appreciation, adds depth to the composition, grounding the portfolio with stability and inflation protection.

A simple yet profound formula for the adolescent investor navigating these waters offers guidance: "100 minus your age." This guideline suggests that the percentage of one's portfolio allocated to stocks should mirror this calculation, with the remainder distributed among bonds, real estate, and other assets. Thus, a 15-year-old should consider a portfolio composed of 85% stocks and 15% spread across bonds and real estate, a composition reflective of the longer investment horizon and higher risk tolerance typically associated with youth. Yet, as with all formulas, flexibility is vital, allowing for adjustments based on individual goals, market conditions, and personal risk appetite.

The voyage into alternative investments beckons as the investor matures, presenting opportunities to diversify further and explore territories marked by higher risks and potential rewards. Commodities, the raw materials that power our world, are a testament to the sector's volatility and significant role in portfolio diversification. Their prices, often inversely related to stocks and bonds, provide a hedge against inflation and economic downturns, their performance shining when traditional assets falter.

Art, a domain where aesthetics meet investment, offers a path that could be more trodden. This realm, where the value is subjectively tied to cultural significance and rarity, presents a unique blend of risk and potential reward. Unlike stocks or bonds, whose worth can be quantified through financial metrics, art's value is deeply intertwined with trends, personal taste, and historical relevance. For the youthful investor, an entry into art investing might begin with acquiring pieces from emerging artists, a venture that holds the promise of appreciation but requires a well-honed sense of market trends and an appreciation for the intangible qualities that define artistic worth.

Balancing a portfolio is akin to navigating a ship through shifting seas. It demands vigilance, an openness to adapt, and an unwavering focus on the distant horizon of financial goals. This endeavor, enriched by the diversity of assets at the investor's disposal, underscores the beauty of investment as a reflection of personal aspiration, risk tolerance, and the ever-evolving landscape of the financial world.

## 6.3 Evaluating and Adjusting Your Portfolio

In the intricate dance of investment, a portfolio once crafted with meticulous care demands continuous scrutiny and nuanced adjustments to thrive amidst the ever-shifting sands of the financial landscape. This vigilance, far from the idle watchfulness of a sentinel, entails a proactive engagement with the assets under one's stewardship, evaluating their performance not merely against the backdrop of market benchmarks but through the lens of personal financial aspirations and the evolving contours of risk tolerance. The act of reviewing and adjusting one's portfolio, thus, transcends the routine maintenance of a financial instrument; it embodies the dynamic recalibration of a strategic vision, ensuring its alignment with the mutable realities of the economic environment and the investor's journey toward fiscal objectives.

The imperative for regular portfolio review emerges from acknowledging that the market and the investor are in perpetual flux. Assets that once harmonized with the investor's goals and risk appetite might, over time, diverge from their intended course, swayed by the tides of market volatility, economic cycles, and the unforeseen tempests of global events. Conversely, the investor, too, may find their goals, circumstances, and tolerance for risk transformed by the passage of time and the accumulation of life experiences. This mutual evolution underscores the necessity of periodic assessments, ensuring that the portfolio faithfully reflects the investor's current financial identity and aspirations.

The rebalancing of a portfolio, thus, emerges as a critical strategy in this endeavor, a deliberate realignment of asset allocations to counteract the drift caused by market movements and shifts in the investor's financial landscape. This recalibration, rooted in asset allocation and diversification principles, requires a discerning eye for the subtle signals of change—in the performance of individual assets, the emergence of new investment opportunities, or the shifting sands of the investor's life goals. Rebalancing strategies, ranging from the disciplined rhythm of calendar rebalancing to the responsive agility of percentage-of-portfolio rebalancing, offer a spectrum of approaches for restoring equilibrium to the portfolio, each tailored to the unique cadence of the investor's financial journey.

Within this framework, the diversification of investments stands as a bulwark against the caprices of the market. This strategy mitigates risk by dispersing investments across various asset classes, sectors, and geographies. This mosaic of investments, carefully curated to reflect the investor's nuanced understanding of risk and return, serves not only as a shield against the volatility of singular assets but as a vessel for capturing the multifarious opportunities presented by the global economy. The continuous diversification of the portfolio, thus, is not merely an exercise in risk management; it is an affirmation of the investor's commitment to a holistic approach to wealth creation, one that embraces the full spectrum of opportunities while guarding against the perils of concentration.

The consideration of tax implications, too, weaves into the fabric of portfolio management, a thread that, though less visible, is integral to the preservation and growth of wealth. The labyrinth of tax laws and regulations, with its potential to erode investment returns, necessitates a strategic approach to investment decisions that seeks to optimize tax efficiency without sacrificing the integrity of the portfolio's strategic vision. This endeavor, balancing the pursuit of after-tax returns with the principles of diversification and risk management, demands a nuanced understanding of the tax implications of various investment vehicles and the judicious use of tax-advantaged accounts and strategies.

Moreover, the vigilant monitoring of fees and expenses associated with investments emerges as a critical component of portfolio management, a recognition that the costs of investing can insidiously undermine the compounding of wealth. In the quest for fiscal efficiency, the investor must navigate the terrain of expense ratios, transaction fees, and advisory costs, seeking pathways that minimize expenses while ensuring access to the requisite tools, advice, and investment opportunities. Though marked by the minutiae of financial products and services, this pursuit is guided by the overarching principle that the value derived from investment services must be commensurate with their cost. This balance optimizes the growth potential of the portfolio.

In this complex interplay of evaluation, rebalancing, and vigilant management of diversification, taxes, and fees, the investor emerges not merely as a steward of wealth but as an architect of their financial destiny. Through the disciplined practice of portfolio review and adjustment, the investor navigates the shifting land-scapes of the market and their personal financial journey, steering their portfolio towards realizing their aspirations. This dynamic and iterative process encapsulates the essence of strategic invest-ment management. This discipline combines the art of financial planning with the science of economic analysis to forge a path toward fiscal growth and stability.

## 6.4 Interactive Element - Diversification Mapping Activity

In the realm where the alchemy of investment transforms the mundane into a portfolio of boundless potential, mapping one's diversification strategy emerges as both a craft and a ritual. This endeavor, far from being a mere exercise in allocation, evolves into an intricate dance with the market's rhythms, a testament to the investor's sagacity and foresight. Here, amid the panoply of assets that the financial world offers, lies the opportunity to weave a tapestry of investments, each strand colored with the hue of a different asset class, each contributing to the strength and resilience of the whole.

Imagine, if you will, a canvas before you, blank and brimming with possibility. This canvas, representing your investment portfolio, awaits the strokes of your colored pencils or markers, each color symbolizing a distinct asset class—stocks in bold crimson, bonds in serene azure, real estate in earthy ochre, and commodities in vibrant green. This activity, the Diversification Mapping Activity, invites you to visually delineate the composition of your portfolio, transforming abstract concepts of asset allocation into a tangible, vivid representation of your financial strategy.

## Crafting Your Diversification Map

Begin by sketching a large circle on your canvas, a mandala within which the art of your investment strategy will unfold. Divide this circle into segments, each corresponding to an asset class you intend to include in your portfolio. The size of each segment will reflect the proportion of your investment dedicated to that asset class, a visual testament to your risk tolerance and financial aspirations.

With your colored pencils or markers ready, infuse each segment with color, painting a visual harmony of diversification. As you color, contemplate the characteristics of each asset class—the growth potential and volatility of stocks, the stability and lower returns of bonds, the tangible value and income generation of real estate, and the inflation hedge offered by commodities. This contemplation, far from a mere intellectual exercise, becomes a meditation on the balance of risk and reward, reflecting the interplay of different investments in achieving your financial goals.

## Guiding Proportions Based on Hypothetical Risk Tolerances

As you craft your diversification map, consider the nuances of your risk tolerance. For those emboldened by youth and a long investment horizon, let the crimson of stocks dominate your canvas, complemented by smaller segments of azure, ochre, and green, mirroring a strategy poised for growth. For investors whose journey has taken them through varied financial landscapes, seeking a balance between development and security, let your mandala reflect a more harmonious blend of colors, with each asset class contributing equally to the composition. And for those who seek the tranquility of stability, let the serene hues of bonds and real estate predominate, accented by the vitality of stocks and commodities.

## Blank Template for Asset Allocation

Accompanying this narrative is a blank template, a starting point for your diversification mapping activity. This template, divided into sections for each asset class, serves as the foundation upon which you will build your personalized investment strategy. As you fill in this template, let your intuition guide the proportions, informed by a keen understanding of your financial landscape and the horizon towards which you navigate.

This activity, a confluence of art and strategy, does more than merely illustrate your diversification approach. It serves as a beacon, guiding your investment decisions through the ebbs and flows of market cycles. It transforms the abstract concept of asset allocation into a tangible, visual strategy you can revisit and revise as your financial journey unfolds.

In this endeavor, you become not just an investor but an artist, a cartographer charting the course of your financial future. The Diversification Mapping Activity, therefore, transcends its utility as a tool for visualizing investment strategy. It becomes a ritual, a rite of passage for the investor who seeks to navigate the markets and understand the deeper rhythms of financial growth and security. Through this activity, the portfolio transforms from a mere collection of assets into reflecting the investor's vision. Each piece and color in this mosaic creates a resilient, flourishing financial future.

## 6.5 Overview & Final Thoughts About this Chapter

Within these pages, a tapestry of strategy and foresight has been woven, illuminating the path for those who seek to safeguard their financial resources and cultivate them with prudence and wisdom. The narrative has unfurled the principles of diversification, a beacon for navigating the tumultuous seas of the financial markets. It ensures that each investment and choice contributes to a resilient portfolio in the face of uncertainty and is ripe with growth potential.

This dialogue has ventured beyond the mere mechanics of distributing assets across various classes, delving into the essence of balance within a portfolio. It has highlighted the necessity of a harmonious blend of investments, each selected to complement and enhance the overall financial strategy. This careful curation, akin to the composition of a symphony, ensures that the crescendos of market highs and the diminuendos of lows resonate with less discord, maintaining the melody of growth and stability.

The discourse has also navigated the intricacies of portfolio evaluation and adjustment, a continuous dance with the ever-evolving landscape of personal financial goals and market dynamics. This process, marked by diligence and adaptability, ensures that the portfolio reflects the investor's aspirations, attuned to economic change and personal evolution rhythms.

The principles detailed in this discourse offer a compass for investments, where the future is a mosaic of possibility and uncertainty. They guide the investor through the variegated terrain of the financial world, ensuring that each step taken is measured and each decision is informed by a deep understanding of risk, reward, and the alchemy of diversification.

As this chapter draws to its close, the narrative does not end. Instead, it transitions, preparing to delve into new realms of financial exploration. The foundation laid here, rooted in the principles of diversification and strategic portfolio management, sets the stage for the next adventure. This forthcoming journey will explore the entrepreneurial spirit that pulses at the heart of the global market, illuminating the paths to investing in startups and private companies. Here, the potential for reward mirrors the spectrum of risk, demanding an approach of courage and caution.

This transition beckons the reader to continue their exploration of the financial landscape, armed with the knowledge and strategies unveiled in the preceding pages. It invites a foray into the world of entrepreneurial investment, a domain where innovation meets opportunity and the principles of diversification and strategic investment find new avenues for application.

In the grand narrative of financial growth and investment, the journey is continuous, each chapter building upon the last, each discovery shedding light on new horizons. The dialogue thus far has equipped the reader with the tools for navigating the present and laid the groundwork for the adventures that lie ahead. In this spirit of continuous exploration and learning, we proceed, ready to uncover the potential in the convergence of entrepreneurship and investment, where the vista of opportunity stretches wide and the promise of the future beckons.

# CHAPTER 7

# ENTREPRENEURIAL VOYAGE:

## INVESTING IN STARTUPS AND PRIVATE COMPANIES

Investing in start-ups and private companies is like getting in on the ground floor of the next big thing. It's where you can help new ideas grow into something tremendous—think about how tech giants like Apple or Facebook started in garages and dorm rooms. Venture capital and angel investing are the two main ways people back these companies, giving them the money they need to turn ideas into reality.

Although these two investment forms are often mentioned together, their essence and approach differ. Venture capital firms are generally involved in the early to mid stages of a start-up's life-cycle. They invest substantial funds in exchange for equity and often have a say in decision-making. On the other hand, Angel investors invest their own money. They are usually involved in the earlier stages of a start-up. They provide smaller amounts of funding in exchange for a share of the company's equity. These entities operate keenly on scalability and market potential, betting on start-ups promising high returns. Angel investors, conversely, enter the fray earlier, sometimes at the nascent idea stage, offering not just capital but mentorship borne out of their own entrepreneurial journeys. These individuals, or groups, invest with a blend of financial foresight and personal conviction, often driven by a belief in the start-up's vision as much as its potential for profitability.

## 7.1 Navigating the Venture Capital Ecosystem

The venture capital ecosystem is driven by innovation, but it has risks. While a few start-ups achieve global success, many need help to live up to their potential. Despite the high stakes, investors are attracted to the possibility of contributing to the next groundbreaking technology or service. The importance of navigating this landscape lies in a careful evaluation process that assesses not just the viability of the business model but also the originality of the idea, the determination of the team, and the start-up's ability to carve out a niche in a competitive market.

### Interactive Element: Venture Evaluation Checklist

A venture evaluation checklist becomes essential in this high-stakes arena to achieve this. Potential investors can use this checklist to analyze a start-up's plan, evaluating factors such as:

- Team Dynamics: Does the team have the technical skills and flexibility needed to manage the challenges of start-up life?
- Market Need: Does the product or service address an unmet need or create a new market entirely?
- Business Model: Does the start-up have a clear path to revenue that promises scalability and sustainability beyond the idea?

- Competitive Landscape: How does the start-up position itself against incumbents and other start-ups within the industry?
- Financial Health: A deep dive into the start-up's financials allows for a detailed analysis of current burn rates and forecasts future profitability and growth.

While not exhaustive, this checklist is a starting point, guiding investors through the labyrinth of considerations that underscore a sound investment decision.

The role of venture capital and angel investing extends beyond the financial injection. These investments are the lifeblood of innovation, propelling start-ups from the ideation phase to market entry and beyond. They are a vote of confidence in the start-up's vision, a signal to the market of its potential, and, crucially, a catalyst for economic growth. By backing start-ups, investors contribute to a vibrant ecosystem where new jobs are created, industries are disrupted, and new markets are forged.

Take, for instance, the journey of a start-up addressing the global water scarcity crisis with a revolutionary purification technology. The initial backing by an angel investor not only validates the technology's potential but also positions the start-up to refine its prototype, secure patents, and initiate pilot projects. As the start-up gains traction, venture capital firms step in, scaling the technology to new markets. In doing so, they generate substantial returns on investment and contribute to addressing a critical global challenge.

**Visual Element: The Start-up Lifecycle Infographic**

A visual representation of the startup lifecycle, annotated with key milestones and the typical entry points for venture capital and angel investments, offers a clear depiction of the growth trajectory and the pivotal role of these investments. This infographic elucidates the journey from concept to market leader, highlighting the phases of seed funding, Series A, B, C rounds, and beyond, culminating in a potential IPO or acquisition. It serves as a roadmap for investors, demystifying the investment process and underscoring the long-term commitment required to shepherd startups to success.

Venture capital and angel investing embody the quintessence of high risk, high reward. It's a domain where foresight, patience, and an unwavering belief in innovation's power converge. For those poised to venture into this realm, the journey promises not just financial returns but the unparalleled gratification of fueling the next wave of innovation that propels society forward. Whether through the strategic deployment of capital in venture funds or the personal mentorship inherent in angel investing, the investments made today are the harbingers of tomorrow's breakthroughs.

## 7.2 Evaluating Startups

The start-up lifecycle involves critical milestones and opportunities for high-risk, high-reward investments. Venture capital and angel investing embody innovation's power, and the investments made today are the key to tomorrow's breakthroughs. By demystifying the investment process and underscoring the long-term commitment required to shepherd start-ups to success, investors can fuel the next wave of innovation and propel society forward. For those willing to venture into this realm, the journey promises financial returns and unparalleled gratification. It's a domain where foresight, patience, and unwavering belief converge, making every investment a step towards making a difference in the world.

Investing in start-ups is a challenging task that requires a combination of analytical skills and intuition. As an investor, you must identify the most promising start-ups from a sea of uncertainty. To do this, you must dive deep into the company's fabric and evaluate its innovation, resilience, market readiness, and scalability.

One critical factor you should consider is the team's composition. The team's synergy, expertise, and vision are essential in igniting the initial spark of possibility. As an investor, you must assess the team's adaptability, cohesion under pressure, and shared drive that propels the start-up forward. You must also evaluate the balance between technical prowess, strategic acumen, and the blend of creative insight and pragmatic execution that characterizes a team poised for success.

The product or service under scrutiny is also crucial in the evaluation process. Its market viability reflects the team's capacity to innovate and execute. You must examine the product's alignment with emergent needs or ability to carve out new desires within the consumer psyche. This exploration should include market research and competitive analysis to uncover the unique value proposition that sets the start-up apart from its competitors.

You also need to consider the start-up's potential market. It is crucial to analyze the growth prospects against the shadows of market saturation, regulatory hurdles, and the ever-looming specter of unforeseen disruptors. This forward-looking analysis aims to gauge the start-up's capacity to scale and transform a niche foothold into a dominant market presence. As an investor, you must be able to identify start-ups that have the potential to succeed and help them achieve their goals.

**Step-by-Step Guide on How to Invest in Start-ups for Teens**

When it comes to starting a business, the way you plan to make money is super important. This is where the business model comes in - it's like a recipe that combines your team, product, and market elements to create a strategy for generating revenue and achieving sustainable growth. Investors want to make sure the model is solid in theory and practice. They'll look at how you plan to make money, how much it'll cost you, how you'll attract and keep customers, and whether you can scale up over time.

If you're a young investor, you might be excited about investing in start-ups. It's a chance to help shape the future! But getting started can be tricky. You'll need to find equity crowdfunding platforms and digital arenas that let you invest and then create an account. This account is your gateway to a whole world of start-ups, each one a new opportunity waiting to be explored.

As you explore different start-ups, balance curiosity and caution. Look for start-ups that align with your values, have potential in the market, and have a product or service that resonates with current trends. But be careful—you must read the fine print carefully before investing. Ensure you know the minimum investment thresholds, how much equity you'll be offered, and your rights as an investor.

Investing in start-ups can be exciting for young investors, but it's a complex process. To get started, you must create an account on an equity crowdfunding platform or digital arena. This will give you access to several start-ups, each with its potential.

When exploring opportunities, it's essential to be curious and cautious. You'll want to look for start-ups that match your values, have potential in the market, and fit in with new trends. You also need to carefully read the terms of engagement, including the minimum investment thresholds, equity offered, and investors' rights.

Investing in a start-up is more than just a transaction—it's a commitment to the company's vision and potential. You'll need to monitor the company's progress and stay engaged with updates on its performance.

Beyond crowdfunding, there are other ways to invest in start-ups, such as creating your own start-up, supporting a friend's venture, or participating in venture capital funds. Each path has its own level of involvement, risk, and potential reward, so you must decide how much you will commit.

**Due Diligence: The Bedrock of Start-up Investment**

Investing in a start-up is a serious task that requires extensive research. The investor must ensure the product is functional, fits the market, and the team is committed to the cause. They must also analyze the market's depth and breadth and examine the start-up's financial health. This includes looking at balance sheets, cash flow statements, and revenue projections to forecast the future trajectory.

Risk assessment is equally important, and the investor needs to examine each potential pitfall to determine its probability and impact on the start-up's journey. This thorough evaluation turns intuition into insight and speculation into strategy. The investor, who is both analytical and visionary, navigates the terrain of start-up investment with a keen eye on the horizon of opportunity. Every step of the investor's life is marked by the dual pursuit of financial returns and transformative impact.

**7.3 Risks and Rewards**

Investing in start-ups is like riding a rollercoaster—thrilling, unpredictable, and full of highs and lows. You could end up backing the next big thing, but there's always a risk it could all fall apart. The potential rewards are enormous, but so are the risks. This makes start-up investing both exciting and nerve-wracking.

The truth is that investing in start-ups is a gamble. Even the most innovative ideas can fail due to competition, operational challenges, or bad timing. But the chance of hitting it big keeps investors coming back. Think about it: some early investors made millions by backing now-famous companies like Facebook and Airbnb when they were just getting started.

Investing in early-stage start-ups is risky because these companies need a proven track record. Investors have to rely on the idea's potential and the founding team's vision. This means putting money into something that might take years to pay off. You have to be patient and okay with being unable to cash out quickly.

But the rewards can go beyond just making money for those who choose wisely. There's something special about being part of a company's growth, helping to shape its direction, and watching it succeed. It's about being part of the entrepreneurial journey and contributing to innovations that could change industries or the world.

It's wise to spread your investments across different start-ups in various industries to balance the risks and rewards. That way, if one fails, the success of others might cover the loss. Venture capital and angel investing are all about taking calculated risks. The key is to do your research and pick investments carefully.

Successful investors aren't just in it for the money; they want to be part of something bigger. They're excited about helping companies grow and make a difference, which makes start-up investing so rewarding!

## 7.4 Interactive Element: The Start-up Investment Simulation

Get ready to dive into start-up investing with this fun and interactive exercise. Imagine you're an investor with the power to back the next big thing. You'll evaluate three fictional start-ups with a unique vision, team, and financial outlook. Your mission is to decide which start-up, if any, you would invest in.

### The Start-up Profiles

AquaInnovate is a company focused on sustainable water purification technologies, led by a team of experienced engineers and environmental scientists. It has a patent-pending filtration system and is starting to partner with municipalities to address water scarcity.

TechTots is an adaptive learning platform for early childhood education. The team includes educators, child psychologists, and software developers. They have promising research results but are still in the early stages of securing widespread adoption.

GreenGrowth is a venture aiming to create rooftop farms on commercial buildings, transforming urban spaces into sustainable food sources. Its team is made up of agronomists, sustainability experts, and real estate veterans. Although it faces challenges with urban planning regulations, it has a vision to change the way cities handle food production.

### The Interactive Exercise

Step into the shoes of an investor and assess each start-up:

- AquaInnovate: Can their technology revolutionize water purification? Do they have the skills to navigate regulatory challenges?

- TechTots: Does their platform have the potential to change early childhood education? Is the market ready for it, despite the financial uncertainties?
- GreenGrowth: Can urban agriculture take off with its innovative approach? Will they be able to overcome zoning laws and other barriers?
- Use a decision tree to guide your evaluation:
- Team: How strong is the team? Do they have the experience and passion needed to succeed?
- Market Fit: Is there a real need for their product or service? How well does it fit into the current market?
- Scalability: Can the business model grow and expand over time?
- Financials: Are their financial projections realistic? Do they have a clear path to profitability?

After carefully considering each start-up, decide where you would invest your money. Reflect on your decisions and write down why you chose the start-up(s) you did.

**Wrapping It Up**

Investing in start-ups is more than just a way to make money; it's about believing in something new and being part of the future. By evaluating these fictional start-ups, you're learning to think like an investor—balancing risk with reward and understanding the importance of thorough research.

This exercise isn't just a game; it's a way to practice making decisions that could one day shape your financial future. So why wait? Jump into this simulation and discover the exciting world of start-up investing!

## 7.5 Overview & Final Thoughts About this Chapter

Venture capital and angel investing shine like bright lights in the world of finance, offering a thrilling path for those passionate about innovation and success. This chapter has guided you through the exciting yet risky landscape of investing in start-ups, helping you spot the difference between ideas with potential and those that might not make it.

Investing in start-ups is more than just putting money into a company—it's about building a partnership where both the investor and the start-up work together toward significant achievements that could change industries or society. This chapter has shown you how to balance risks with the chance for huge rewards strategically, inspiring you to aim for financial growth while supporting innovation.

This chapter also explains how to evaluate start-ups, giving you a toolkit to dig deeper into a company's potential. From analyzing the team and their vision to understanding the market and product, you now have a framework to make informed decisions. It's not just about the numbers; it's about seeing the bigger picture and believing in the start-up's journey, which will give you a deeper understanding and insight into the investment process.

The risks and rewards of start-up investing are undeniably real. This chapter has shown you that while the stakes are high, the potential for returns is equally impressive. The key is approaching it with optimism and caution, using portfolio diversification to spread your investments across different start-ups and industries. This understanding will make you feel the gravity of the situation and the potential for impressive returns.

The interactive simulation, a key feature of this chapter, allowed you to practice being an investor, applying what you've learned to real-world scenarios. This hands-on activity was designed to make the concepts you've studied come to life, turning theory into action. It also encouraged you to reflect on your investment philosophy, helping you understand what kind of investor you want to be. The simulation involved making virtual investments in hypothetical start-ups, tracking their progress, and making decisions based on the outcomes.

**Actions to Apply Your Knowledge:**

1. Explore Equity Crowdfunding Platforms: Start by signing up on Seedrs, Crowdcube, or Republic. These platforms allow you to browse various start-ups and learn about their business models, teams, and market potential.
2. Practice Due Diligence: Choose a start-up that interests you and research it thoroughly. Look into the team's background, the product they're developing, and how they plan to make money. Write down your thoughts and decide whether you would invest in this start-up.
3. Create a Mock Portfolio: Use a spreadsheet to create a mock portfolio of start-ups you would invest in. Track their progress over time, noting any developments or news about the companies. This exercise will help you understand how start-ups evolve and how your investment decisions play out.
4. Engage in Start-up Communities: Join online forums or local groups where entrepreneurs and investors discuss start-up ideas and investment strategies. Engaging with these communities will give you insights into the start-up ecosystem and help you build connections with like-minded individuals.

As we move forward, the next chapter will focus on something every investor needs to understand—debt management and credit building. These are the building blocks of financial stability; mastering them will empower you to make intelligent decisions in all areas of your financial life. By bridging the exciting world of start-up investing with the practical knowledge of managing debt and credit, you'll be better prepared for a future where financial wisdom and sustainability come together.

# CHAPTER 8

# THE ART OF WAR ON DEBT:

## ADVANCED DEBT MANAGEMENT
## AND CREDIT BUILDING

Debt can be a powerful force in one's financial life, either helping or hindering growth, depending on how it's managed. It's crucial to differentiate between beneficial and detrimental debt to make the most of it. Understanding this distinction is essential to achieving financial stability and unlocking wealth-building opportunities.

Navigating debt is like deciphering a complex code that, when unlocked, reveals pathways to financial empowerment. It's not just about avoiding debt but strategically using it as a tool for advancement. This chapter aims to equip you with the knowledge to differentiate between 'good' and 'bad' debt and to use the former to its fullest potential, ensuring a robust financial foundation.

To understand the battlefield of good and bad debt, it is necessary to examine the blurred line that divides them. Good debt includes loans for education, real estate, or business ventures—investments that promise future returns or value appreciation. For example, a mortgage for a home in a growing neighborhood or student loans for education in high-demand fields exemplifies good debt. These are investments in your future, expected to increase your financial worth over time.

On the other hand, lousy debt undermines financial stability without offering tangible returns. High-interest credit cards and loans for depreciating assets, such as an expensive car model that loses value when it leaves the showroom, typify lousy debt. This type of debt, hazardous due to high-interest rates, can quickly become a financial quagmire, swallowing resources that could have been allocated towards investments or savings.

## 8.1 Strategic Use of Good Debt: Paving Paths to Wealth

Imagine considering a loan to pay for college or buy a house. These are examples of good debt because they're investments in your future. Similarly, a business loan to start a profitable venture or a mortgage to buy a property in a growing neighborhood could be considered good debt. On the other hand, bad debt is like buying things that lose value quickly, like an expensive car, or piling up credit card debt on stuff you don't need. This type of debt can weigh you down, making it harder to save money or invest in things that matter.

On the other hand, bad debt is like buying things that lose value quickly, like an expensive car, or piling up credit card debt on stuff you don't need. This type of debt can weigh you down, making it harder to save money or invest in things that matter.

### Visual Element: Debt Decision Tree

Before taking on debt, use a decision tree to help you think it through. Ask yourself questions like:

- What is the purpose of this loan?
- Will it help me grow financially?
- Can I realistically afford the payments?

This decision tree will help you see whether taking on debt is a smart move or if it might lead to financial trouble.

## Leveraging Good Debt: Real Estate and Education

Good debt can be a powerful tool when used strategically to build wealth. For example:

- Real Estate: Investing in property located in a growing area can appreciate over time, turning into a substantial asset.
- Education: Taking out student loans to pursue a degree in a high-demand field can open doors to higher-paying job opportunities.

Just as a gardener carefully selects seeds to plant for a future harvest, you should choose debts that have the potential to help you grow financially. By making informed decisions about which debts to take on, you can set yourself up for long-term success.

## Everyday Strategies for Managing Debt

Picture this: You're at a crossroads. One path leads to raising high-interest credit card debt, and the other leads to a well-planned student loan that can advance your career. It's all about making intelligent choices. Even small decisions, like saving up for something instead of charging it to a credit card, can make a big difference in your financial future. You can confidently make these choices with the knowledge and tools provided in this chapter.

**Interactive Element: Monthly Debt Management Plan**

Create a monthly debt management plan to help you manage your debts and make timely payments. List all your debts, their interest rates, and minimum payments. Prioritize paying off high-interest debt first while keeping up with good debt, like student loans.

This plan will help you take control of your finances, allowing you to progress toward becoming debt-free while investing in your future.

## 8.2 Negotiating Debt Terms

Negotiating debt terms can help ease the burden of loans with high interest or unfavorable conditions. Here's how to do it:

- Do Your Homework: Gather all the details about your current debt, including interest rates and payment schedules. This will help you make a strong case for better terms.
- Know Your Financial Situation: Understand your income, expenses, and financial goals so you can realistically assess what you can afford.
- Create a Solid Proposal: When negotiating with lenders, present a clear plan for repaying the debt under new terms. Back it up with financial projections to show you're serious.
- Shop Around: Check out other lending institutions to see if they offer better terms. This gives you leverage when negotiating with your current lender.
- Be Willing to Compromise: Negotiation is a two-way street. Be open to meeting your lender halfway to reach a mutually beneficial agreement.

- Techniques for Negotiation: Script Examples

When talking to your lender, keep it respectful and professional. Start by acknowledging the existing agreement, then explain your current situation and propose new terms.

**Example Script:**

"Hi, thanks for discussing my loan terms with me. I've reviewed my finances and would like to explore adjusting my interest rate or repayment period to match my current financial situation better. I've been making payments consistently and remain committed to fulfilling my obligations. I believe [proposed condition] would be more manageable for me. Can we discuss working together to find a solution that benefits us?"

**Success Stories: Triumphs in Debt Negotiation**

Real people have successfully negotiated better debt terms, leading to financial freedom. For example, one person struggling with credit card debt negotiated lower interest rates, making it easier to pay off. Another individual, after a divorce, was able to work with creditors to reduce financial strain and regain stability.

These stories show you can turn your financial situation around with persistence and intelligent negotiation.

**8.3 Credit Building Strategies**

Credit scores are like report cards for your financial life. They can determine how easily you can borrow money and at what cost. Understanding how credit scores work is critical to using them to your advantage.

Credit scores change based on your financial decisions. They're calculated by looking at things like your payment history and how much of your available credit you're using. Regularly monitoring your credit score and understanding what impacts it can help you make better financial choices.

**Tools for Building Credit**

Secured Credit Cards: These cards require a deposit, making them a safe way to build or rebuild credit.

Credit-Builder Loans: These loans disburse funds after you make regular payments, helping you build credit while saving money.

Using credit responsibly means balancing what you spend with what you can afford to pay off each month. Regularly check your credit report for errors and dispute any inaccuracies to keep your score as high as possible.

## 8.4 Interactive Element: Crafting a Map to Navigate Through Seas of Debt

Managing debt is like navigating rough waters. It's not just about listing your debts; it's about analyzing each to see how it impacts your financial health.

**The Worksheet: A Beacon in the Fog**

Use a worksheet to track your debts, including how much you owe, the interest rates, and the monthly payments. Consider the interest rates and balances owed to prioritize which debts to pay off first. High-interest debts should be tackled first, while low-interest debts can be handled over time.

This worksheet isn't just about writing down numbers; it's a map to guide you through your financial journey.

Tracking Progress: Charting a Course Through Stormy Seas

Use your worksheet to track your progress toward paying off debt. Make it a living document that you update regularly. Reflect on your journey and adjust as needed to stay on course toward financial freedom.

This approach turns debt management into a strategic journey, helping you move closer to financial stability.

## 8.5 Overview & Final Thoughts About this Chapter

In this chapter, we've delved into the intricacies of debt management and credit building, equipping you with the knowledge and tools to navigate these critical aspects of personal finance. By understanding the difference between good and bad debt, you gain the power to make informed decisions that pave the way for financial growth rather than hindrance. Whether leveraging good debt for investments in real estate or education, negotiating better terms on existing loans, or strategically building your credit, you now have the foundation to manage your financial future with confidence.

As you move forward, remember that managing debt and building credit is not just about numbers - they're about making choices that align with your long-term goals, building a solid credit score, and a foundation of limitless prosperity. The strategies discussed in this chapter are designed to empower you to take control of your financial journey, turning potential obstacles into opportunities for growth and prosperity.

The following section will give you two powerful bonuses to kick-start your financial journey. You will take on year-long challenges to help you manage debt, build credit, and prepare you to grow your savings and investment portfolio. These practical steps will build upon your lessons, ensuring you are aware of financial strategies and actively applying them to achieve long-term success. With these tools, you will be well-equipped to continue your path toward economic independence and make meaningful progress toward your goals.

# CONCLUSION

As we near the end of our investment journey in A Teenager Learning About Financial Literacy, it's a perfect time to reflect on our exciting adventure and the significant progress we've made together. Here's a recap of what we covered in the different chapters, a testament to your dedication and eagerness to learn. Remember, the key to long-term success is being a steady, constant learner—always ready to adapt, grow, and deepen your understanding. Keep this mindset, and you'll continue to thrive in your financial journey and beyond.

Chapter One introduced you to the fascinating world of behavioral finance, emphasizing the critical role of emotions in investing. By exploring strategies for emotional discipline and developing a growth mindset, you learned how to navigate the turbulent waters of financial markets. The chapter also delved into the impact of peer influence and provided tools for mindful investing, empowering you to make informed decisions aligned with your financial goals. This foundational knowledge sets the stage for your journey toward financial independence.

Chapter Two gave you an exciting exploration of cryptocurrencies and blockchain technology. You understood how blockchain works and the high risks and rewards associated with digital currencies. Practical guidance on getting started with cryptocurrency investments helped you navigate this volatile yet promising market. The chapter also addressed the ethical and social implications of digital currencies, prompting you to consider the broader impact of your investment choices.

Chapter Three broadened your horizons by introducing you to international markets and the global economy. You learned the basics of global investing, the significance of economic indicators, and how technology shapes global markets. Through an interactive investment quiz, you developed the skills to analyze global dynamics and make informed decisions about international investments. This chapter taught you to participate confidently in the worldwide economy.

Chapter Four was a discovery of the growing field of Socially Responsible Investing (SRI) and Environmental, Social, and Governance (ESG) investing. You explored the visible benefits of ESG investments and learned how to evaluate and select ethical investment opportunities. By crafting your ethical portfolio, you can align your financial goals with your values, demonstrating that investing can be profitable and purposeful.

Chapter Five introduced you to real estate investing, focusing on Real Estate Investment Trusts (REITs). You learned why REITs are valuable to your investment portfolio and how to evaluate crowdfunding real estate projects. The chapter also provided advanced strategies for crafting a diversified real estate portfolio, enabling you to confidently and precisely navigate the real estate market.

Chapter Six emphasized the importance of diversification for your portfolio and taught you how to balance and adjust your investment portfolio. You learned the significance of spreading your investments across different asset classes to manage risk and maximize returns. With an interactive diversification mapping activity, you developed a personalized strategy for growing wealth through a well-balanced portfolio.

Chapter Seven introduced the exciting world of investing in start-ups and private companies. You explored the venture capital ecosystem, a complex but rewarding landscape. By understanding how to evaluate start-ups and the risks and rewards associated with early-stage investments, you gained the confidence to make investment decisions that could shape the future of innovative companies.

Chapter Eight concluded our journey with advancing debt management and credit building. We learned that debt can be a double-edged sword—a stepping stone to wealth or a pitfall leading to financial instability. By distinguishing between good and bad debt, you must find your best personal strategy to use as your powerful tool for economic advancement. Remember how important it is to maintain a strong credit score, a key to unlocking future financial opportunities and ensuring debt works for you, not against you, as you continue your journey toward financial success. Try your best to simplify your personal investing, making it a captivating and enjoyable journey. We sought to instill a belief that financial independence is not just a distant dream, but a tangible reality within your reach, provided you arm yourself with knowledge, maintain discipline, and actively manage your finances.

The central lesson from our time together is clear: investing is more than just about growing your wealth—it's a potent tool for empowering yourself to make informed choices, comprehend the actual value of money, and utilize your resources wisely to shape a prosperous future. Each chapter, story, and activity in this book was meticulously crafted to lead you toward becoming not just an investor but a savvy one armed with the tools and insights to conquer the financial world that awaits you.

As we part ways in this book, let's draw inspiration from the story of Maya—a teenager who, guided by the principles we've discussed, delved into investing with naught but a smartphone and a zealous thirst for knowledge. She took simple steps, set clear goals, and commenced with small investments. Today, Maya's burgeoning portfolio is a testament to the power of commencing early and growing steadfastly, reflecting the transformation we aspire for you.

Now, the ball's in your court. Take that crucial first step from this book—downloading an investment app, delving into real estate investment trusts, or sharing your financial goals. Your expedition commences with that very first stride. Remember, this book signifies not the end but the inception of your financial education. Keep learning, stay inquisitive, and always strive to broaden your horizons. Investing in financial literacy and personal development will reap bountiful rewards for your future self, enriching your mind and life.

As we draw this journey together to an end, I implore you to share your thoughts and experiences about this book. Your insights and stories as an emerging investor are of immeasurable value. Share your journey on social media or through our book's website to unite with a community dedicated to growth and learning. And if this book has ignited a new curiosity or drive in you, contemplate leaving a review on Amazon to reinforce our mission that inspires other young individuals to embark on their financial journey.

Remember that the world is teeming with boundless opportunities as you venture forth. Armed with knowledge and determination, the treasures you can unearth are limitless. Here's to your triumphant stride in investing and beyond! And recall, another book in this series awaits to aid you in continuing your journey, further expanding your horizons. Embrace it as your next stride toward mastering the realm of finance. Happy investing!

## SPREAD YOUR LIGHT AND INSPIRE OTHERS

Did this book inspire or challenge you? If so, your review can be the light that guides someone else toward financial transformation. Just like one flame lights a thousand candles, your words could help a future entrepreneur or a young dreamer take their first step toward financial freedom.

It only takes a minute to make a lasting impact. How?

Simply **scan the QR code below** to leave a review.

Your kind words could give someone the confidence to start their journey toward financial prosperity.

Thank you for being part of this adventure. We're all in this together!

**Forever grateful, Chad**

# REFERENCES

Investing for Teens: What They Should Know https://online.mason.wm.edu/blog/what-is-behavioral-finance

These Two Examples Illustrate the Magic of Compound Interest https://www.figmarketing.com/blog/the-psychology-of-financial-decision-making-understanding-behavioral-biases-and-improving-client-outcomes/.

Stocks, Bonds, And Mutual Funds: Key Differences https://www.timevaluemillionaire.com/behavioral-finance-concepts

What is the stock market? | A guide for teens - Greenlight https://www.wallstreetmojo.com/behavioral-finance/

'SMART' Financial Goal-setting | Wharton Global Youth Program https://usa.kaspersky.com/resource-center/definitions/what-is-cryptocurrency

23 Best Money Apps for Teens https://www.coindesk.com/learn/what-is-bitcoin/

Saving vs. Investing: Understanding the Key Differences https://www.forbes.com/advisor/investing/cryptocurrency/top-10-cryptocurrencies/

How to create a financial goals vision board that works ... https://aevi.com/newsroom/payments-landscape/cryptocurrency-mainstream-payment-method

Best investment accounts for kids 2024 https://www.uschamber.com/international/the-benefits-of-international-investment

What is Micro-Investing, and How Do I Start? | Stash Learn https://www.winvesta.in/blog/benefits-and-risk-of-global-investing

5 Apps To Help Teens Start Investing https://www.hartfordfunds.com/practice-management/client-conversations/investing-for-growth/10-things-you-should-know-about-international-investing.html

Fundamental vs. Technical Analysis: What's the Difference? https://www.forbes.com/advisor/in/investing/a-beginners-guide-to-investing-globally/

Types of investment risk https://www.investopedia.com/terms/s/sri.asp

Meet the 17-year-old investor who tripled his money https://esgclarity.com/companies-with-higher-esg-ratings-see-stronger-investment-returns/

How to Invest in Cryptocurrency - Investopedia https://www.investopedia.com/terms/r/reit.asp

REITs 101: A Beginner's Guide to Real Estate Investment Trusts https://fundrise.com/education/reits-101-a-beginners-guide-to-real-estate-investment-trusts

Ethical Investing: Overview and How To Do It - Investopedia https://www.reit.com/what-reit/types-reits

Why ETF Investing Is Ideal for Young Investors https://www.reit.com/investing/financial-benefits-reits

Stimulate Your Skills With Simulated Trading https://www.investopedia.com/investing/importance-diversification

23 Best Money Apps for Teens https://time.com/personal-finance/article/importance-of-diversification/

Social Media Investment Scams https://www.fidelity.com/learning-center/investment-products/mutual-funds/diversification

2024 Financial Services Predictions: AI, Blockchain, ESG, ... https://www.inc.com/sujan-patel/10-smart-entrepreneurs-that-diversified-with-multiple-income-streams.html

How to Reach Financial Independence Early in 8 Steps https://www.equifax.com/personal/education/credit/report/articles/-/learn/understanding-credit-good-debt-vs-bad-debt/

Teen Author Inspires Young Investors with New Book https://www.fultonbank.com/Education-Center/Managing-Credit-and-Debt/How-to-create-good-debt-and-steer-clear-of-bad-debt.

Financial Literacy: What It Is, and Why It Is So Important to ... https://www.fidelity.com/learning-center/smart-money/good-debt-vs-bad-debt

10 Strategies to Avoid Getting into Debt https://www.deltafinancialgroup.com.au/7-powerful-ways-to-use-debt-to-build-wealth/

Investing guide for teens: Skills, account types & tips to know https://boardclic.com/blog/social-metrics

Beginners' Guide to Financial Statement https://www.unpri.org/asset-owner-resources/asset-owner-strategy-guide-how-to-craft-an-investment-strategy/402.article

Investment Clubs for Teens Are a Fast-Growing Trend https://corporatefinanceinstitute.com/resources/esg/esg-environmental-social-governance/

Factors That Cause the Market to Go Up and Down https://www.knowesg.com/featured-article/5-tips-to-attract-youth-esg-investment

www.ingramcontent.com/pod-product-compliance
Lightning Source LLC
Chambersburg PA
CBHW030311130626
46549CB00002B/797